RELIGION IN SCHOOLS: LEARNING LESSONS FROM WALES

To what extent should religion be taught in classrooms? Should lessons also cover non-religious beliefs? Should the teaching of religion be compulsory or should it be a matter of choice by the parents or the child? Should faith schools be allowed to teach their religious beliefs? Should religious worship be compulsory for all pupils?

Questions of how religion operates within schools prove controversial and divisive. This book explores the historical development of the law on these matters in England and Wales before exploring the radical changes that are being made in Wales and the lessons that can be learnt from them for elsewhere, especially England where the law remains in its unreformed state. Part one of the book uncovers how the law on religion in schools has been the product of historical compromises that reflected the social and religious nature of their times and reveals that the explicit reference to Christianity was a very late addition. Requirements that religious education syllabuses must reflect 'the fact that the religious traditions in Great Britain are in the main Christian' and that daily 'collective worship shall be wholly or mainly of a broadly Christian character' date back only to the time of the Thatcher Government.

Part two of the book explores how the Curriculum and Assessment (Wales) Act 2021 introduces a new curriculum for Wales and makes the teaching of Religion, Values and Ethics compulsory for all. As the name of the new subject suggests, the study of non-religious beliefs will now be explicitly included and groups such as humanists will play a role in the writing of the curriculum. The book provides a legislative history of what was to become the 2021 Act and examines the author's own contributions to Welsh Parliament debates on the matter. The 2021 Act will mean that the law on the teaching of religion in Wales will differ from England for the first time. This book will explore what can be learnt from developments in Wales and whether the reforms go far enough.

Russell Sandberg is Professor of Law at Cardiff University. His research interrogates the interaction between law and humanities, with particular reference to Law and Religion and Legal History. He is the author of *Law and Religion* (Cambridge University Press, 2011), *Religion, Law and Society* (Cambridge University Press, 2014), *Subversive Legal History* (Routledge, 2021) and *Religion and Marriage Law: The Need for Reform* (Bristol University Press, 2021). He is the editor of the Anthem Studies in Law Reform.

Religion in Schools

Religion in Schools
Learning Lessons from Wales

Russell Sandberg

ANTHEM PRESS

Anthem Press
An imprint of Wimbledon Publishing Company
www.anthempress.com

This edition first published in UK and USA 2022
by ANTHEM PRESS
75–76 Blackfriars Road, London SE1 8HA, UK
or PO Box 9779, London SW19 7ZG, UK
and
244 Madison Ave #116, New York, NY 10016, USA

Copyright © Russell Sandberg 2022

The author asserts the moral right to be identified as the author of this work.

All rights reserved. Without limiting the rights under copyright reserved above, no part of this publication may be reproduced, stored or introduced into a retrieval system, or transmitted, in any form or by any means (electronic, mechanical, photocopying, recording or otherwise), without the prior written permission of both the copyright owner and the above publisher of this book.

British Library Cataloguing-in-Publication Data
A catalogue record for this book is available from the British Library.

Library of Congress Control Number: 2022932341

ISBN-13: 978-1-83998-425-9 (Pb)
ISBN-10: 1-83998-425-2 (Pb)

This title is also available as an e-book.

To Emma, with love.

CONTENTS

Acknowledgments	xi
1. Introduction	1
Part One RELIGIOUS EDUCATION AND WORSHIP UNDER ENGLISH LAW	**5**
2. The Position before the Butler Act	7
3. The Butler Act	17
4. The Position after the Butler Act	27
5. The Current Law	37
6. The Human Rights Context	47
Part Two THE NEW WELSH LAW ON RELIGION, VALUES AND ETHICS	**51**
7. The New Curriculum for Wales	53
8. The Consultation Phase	59
9. The Curriculum and Assessment (Wales) Bill	75
10. The Passage of the Bill	83
11. The New Law	93
12. Conclusion	107
Bibliography	111
Index	115

ACKNOWLEDGMENTS

I was fortunate to have study leave in the academic year 2020–21 to complete works on two books, which became *Religion and Marriage Law: The Need for Reform* and *Subversive Legal History: A Manifesto for the Future of Legal Education*.[1] However, during the period of study leave, another legal development took my attention: what was to become the Curriculum and Assessment (Wales) Act 2021. This ushered in the new Curriculum for Wales complete with a new radical approach to the teaching of religion in schools in Wales. These changes quickly went from consultation to legislation, and so during my study leave I responded to a number of consultations, penned several briefings that I sent to Welsh politicians and wrote a number of blog posts on the developments (on my own website *http://sandberglaw.wordpress.com* and for Law and Religion UK, *http://lawandreligionuk.com*, the leading blog on the subject run by Frank Cranmer and David Pocklington).

It was also during my study leave that I had a conversation with Megan Greiving at Anthem Press about their new Impact programme for short books and the opportunities this afforded for Law scholars. Out of this conversation emerged our new *Anthem Studies in Law Reform* book series, which seeks to bridge the gap between legal activism and academic scholarship by publishing work that is too short and policy-focused to become an academic monograph but is also too long and practically orientated to be a journal article. In setting up the series, I had not intended to write for it but when the Curriculum and Assessment (Wales) Act 2021 received Royal Assent and became law, I began to think that the story about how the law on religion in schools in Wales was now diverging from the law in England needed to be told in a more concrete and considered form than in the blog posts; how there was need to explore the strengths and weaknesses, opportunities and risks of the new Welsh approach and whether England (and indeed other countries)

---

1 Russell Sandberg, *Religion and Marriage Law: The Need for Reform* (Bristol University Press, 2021) and Russell Sandberg, *Subversive Legal History: A Manifesto for the Future of Legal Education* (Routledge, 2021).

should now follow the precedent set by Wales. It soon became apparent that this fitted with the aims of the new Anthem series and the result became the book that you currently have in your hands.

The other books that I worked on during the academic year 2020–21 have undoubtedly influenced the writing of this one. This book can be seen as a companion of sorts to *Religion and Marriage Law: The Need for Reform* in that both books are about the need to reform areas in which the law interacts with religion where the legal framework is archaic. Now that blasphemy has been abolished, English marriage law and education law provide the clearest examples of laws recognising and giving special treatment to Christianity, in general, or the Church of England, in particular. Other parts of the legal framework now tend to recognise and regulate religion or religion or belief more generally. In both the education and marriage law contexts, the law feels out of step with social practices and values.

Yet, when writing this book, I was also struck by the impact that had been made by researching and writing *Subversive Legal History: A Manifesto for the Future of Legal Education*. That book argued that history should be at the beating heart of legal scholarship and legal education. It discussed how reference to history rebuts the way in which every generation thinks that the challenges they face are unique. This argument can also be found in the present book, which took on a more historical perspective while I was writing it. During my research, it became clear that the debates that occurred in the Welsh Senedd in 2020 had echoes throughout the centuries. It is the same rain. This could animate a sense of futility, of going around in circles. Yet, I find this encouraging. For me, it shows that there is more than one solution, that there are different possibilities and that there is a need to reshape the law to fit the changing social and intellectual context. While writing this book, I was constantly reminded of the words of Frederic W Maitland, the patron saint of legal history who once wrote that:

> The only direct utility of legal history … lies in the lesson that each generation has an enormous power of shaping its own law. I don't think that the study of legal history would make men fatalists; I doubt that it would make them conservatives. I am sure that it would free them from superstitions and teach them that they have free hands.[2]

---

2 Frederic W. Maitland, 'Maitland to AV Dicey, c. July 1896' quoted in C H S Fifoot, *Frederic William Maitland* (Harvard University Press, 1971), 143.

In writing this book, it also became apparent that education law did not provide an example of linear secularisation or of what is often viewed as progress. The religiosity found in the current law in England, which the 2021 Act diverges from in some respects in Wales, is actually the product of political choices made mostly in the 1940s which were buttressed considerably in the late 1980s. They are of comparatively recent origin. This book examines the Curriculum and Assessment (Wales) Act 2021 and its likely effect, looking to the future, but seeks to understand the legislation by looking at the past. It is also an account of a moving target: although the Act has been passed, implementation is forthcoming and its effects are still yet to be seen.

Although this book will argue that there is much unfinished business and areas where the Act has not been radical enough, it broadly welcomes the Curriculum and Assessment (Wales) Act 2021 as a much-needed attempt to modernise an outdated and outmoded legal framework that had failed to keep up with societal changes. The Welsh Government and Senedd have truly grasped the powers in their hands to transform the law on education, freeing teachers and pupils to develop ways of educating and thinking that are necessary in the twenty-first century. Particularly commendable is the inclusion of non-religious beliefs which sees education law in Wales catch up with human rights and discrimination law provisions that protect freedom of religion or belief. Although there are risks with the new approach, it nevertheless marks an important step forward, ensuring that the next generation of Welsh citizens are religiously literate, being not only tolerant of religious differences but also champions of freedoms of thought and conscience, religion or belief. There is much other nations (not least England) can learn from the Welsh transformation.

In writing this book, I have also learnt a great deal from others. My interest in the law on religion and education has been longstanding and has been the focus of several chapters and articles over many years, beginning with the chapter on the topic in *Law and Religion*.[3] I am grateful to all who have helped me in the writings of those pieces, those I have discussed the matters with and those students who I have taught over the years. I am especially grateful to Frank Cranmer and David Pocklington who over the last couple of years have published a number of guest posts from me on this topic on their blog that have allowed me to develop my thinking on the matter and engage with others. I am thankful to Professor Norman Doe, Professor Mark Hill QC and

---

3 Russell Sandberg, *Law and Religion* (Cambridge University Press, 2011).

Christopher Grout, my co-authors on *Religion and Law in the United Kingdom*,[4] especially because updating the section on religious education for the third edition of that book impressed on me how radical the changes then mooted for Wales would be. I am also grateful to Dr Sharon Thompson for countless conversations about the text and her infectious encouragement. I am indebted to Megan Greiving and the team at Anthem Press for their professional commitment to the book. As always, my greatest thanks go to my family and to my partner Emma. It is fitting that this short book on education in Wales has been written in a home lived in by two educators in Wales; it is unfortunate, however, that it has not been penned by the most committed, thoughtful and intelligent educator of the two.

Russell Sandberg
Neath, South Wales
January 2022

---

4 Mark Hill QC, Russell Sandberg, Norman Doe and Christopher Grout, *Religion and Law in the United Kingdom* (3rd ed., Kluwer Law International, 2021).

Chapter 1

INTRODUCTION

The year 2020 will always be remembered as the year the Covid pandemic hit. As with other pandemics throughout history,[1] Covid-19 has already had significant economic, social, political and legal effects. Some effects will take time before they can be seen clearly, but one significant effect of the 2020 Covid pandemic in the United Kingdom that is already visible has been the strengthening of the devolved powers in Scotland, Wales and Northern Ireland. Since health was a devolved matter, increased attention was shone on the leaders and legislators of Edinburgh, Cardiff and Belfast as the various nations of the United Kingdom dealt with Covid differently.

However, another significant change also occurred in Wales in 2020 in regard to a different devolved matter. While grappling with Covid, Wales' politicians were also debating and legislating for a brand new curriculum for Wales' schools. The result, the Curriculum and Assessment (Wales) Act 2021, will transform the education sector and the ways in which children will be taught. It is the most radical change for at least thirty years and is probably the most significant Act passed by the Welsh Senedd to date.

This is particularly true regarding the place of religion in schools in Wales. Previously, schools in Wales followed the same law as schools in England. Now in Wales, Religious Education will be renamed Religion, Values and Ethics. Parents will no longer have the right to opt their children out of these lessons. The way in which syllabuses will be written will change with humanist and non-religious organisations playing a greater role, with schools having more freedom and with more Wales-wide guidance. The Act's provisions will also apply to so-called faith schools in Wales: specific rules will apply to schools with a religious character to ensure that they seek to strike a balance between the schools operating in a way that, on the one hand, reflects their

---

1 On the impact of the Black Death, for instance, see Robert C. Palmer, *English Law in the Age of the Black Death 1348-1381: A Transformation of Governance and Law* (University of North Carolina Press, 1993) and Mark Bailey, *After the Black Death: Economy, Society and the Law in Fourteenth Century England* (Oxford University Press, 2021).

ethos and the rights of parents and, on the other, ensures that children receive pluralistic teaching on religion if they so wish.

This book tells the story of how Wales is transforming how religion is taught in its schools and asks what lessons can be learned. These lessons do not only apply in England where the law is still the same as it used to be in Wales but also further afield. I argue that the changes ushered in by the Curriculum and Assessment (Wales) Act 2021 are to be broadly welcomed. They reform an antiquated legal framework that is no longer fit for purpose in the twenty-first century. However, in some respects, the Welsh reforms are not quite bold enough. This is particularly true in relation to the continued existence of bodies at local authority level (Standing Advisory Councils) and the provisions on schools with a religious character. Moreover, the reform of the law on religious education leaves untouched the law on religious worship, which is as outdated as the old law on religious education if not more so. The message of this book is that England and other countries should follow Wales' lead in introducing a law on religion in schools that is modern, clear and equal. However, there remains a need for further reform and improvement in order for the law to truly reflect the social reality.

This short book falls into two parts. The first part examines 'Religious Education under English Law'. This adopts a historical approach. It begins with an introduction to the origins of the law in England and Wales (Chapter 2) before focusing on the seminal mid-twentieth century legislation on the matter, the Butler Act 1944 (Chapter 3) before moving on to discuss later developments that are often overlooked (Chapter 4). A summary of the current law will then be provided (Chapter 5). This part concludes with a brief examination of the international law provisions that also developed from the 1940s onwards which affect the regulation of freedom of religion, the right to education and the rights of parents (Chapter 6). These international norms and societal changes have animated concerns that the current law on religious education in England is outmoded and may not be fully compatible with the human right to freedom of religion or belief.

The second part, 'The New Welsh Law on Religion, Values and Ethics', provides the first account of how the teaching of religion is being reformed in Wales. It again adopts a historical perspective providing a legislative history of the changes that are now to be found in the Curriculum and Assessment (Wales) Act 2021. It begins with a brief introduction to the role and legislative competence of what is now the Welsh Senedd (also known as the Welsh Parliament) and a discussion of the proposals for a new Curriculum for Wales generally (Chapter 7). It will then examine the initial consultations on the teaching of religion and the Welsh Government's response to this (Chapter 8). The focus will then move on to examine in detail the development of the

Curriculum and Assessment (Wales) Bill beginning with exploring its content (Chapter 9). The Bill's passage through the Welsh Senedd will then be examined, exploring how the provisions on religious education proved controversial and highlighting my criticisms of the Act as passed including discussion of how my criticisms were quoted and discussed in the final Parliamentary debate (Chapter10). This part concludes with a summary of the new law and an analysis of the published guidance (Chapter 11).

The final chapter takes the form of a conclusion that explores the unfinished business left by the Act not only in terms of its deficiencies but also in terms of the law on religious worship, which is unaffected by the 2021 Act and so continues to apply in England and Wales (Chapter 12).

Part One

RELIGIOUS EDUCATION AND WORSHIP UNDER ENGLISH LAW

Richard Austen Butler (familiarly known as Rab from his initials) often appears on lists of the greatest Prime Ministers that the United Kingdom never had. Rab was Education Minister during World War II and successively Chancellor of the Exchequer, Home Secretary, Deputy Prime Minister and Foreign Secretary during the Macmillan and Douglas-Home Conservative Governments. He is best known, however, for the Education Act 1944 which is commonly called the 'Butler Act'. This Act introduced free secondary schooling for all through a tripartite system: pupils were graded by an 'eleven-plus' exam into three intellectual groups for specific types of school – grammar, secondary modern and technical. The Butler Act provided for compulsory Religious Instruction (RI) and worship in all schools which received State funding, though parents could withdraw children on grounds of conscience. The Act also recognised Standing Advisory Councils for Religious Education (SACREs): regulatory bodies at a local authority level that developed local syllabuses. This laid the foundations of the law on religion in schools that continues to operate in England (and operates in Wales until the reforms in the 2021 Act take effect). The roots of the law on religious education, therefore, have much in common with the solution to many murder mysteries in popular culture; in both cases, Butler did it.

However, the history of religious education did not begin in the 1940s. This part places the achievements of Rab Butler in context.[1] It employs a historical approach to examine current law on religious education and religious

---

1 It focuses on the legal framework on religion rather than changing policies and approaches to the teaching of religion on which see Terence Copley, *Teaching Religion* (2nd ed, University of Exeter Press, 2008) and Alan Brine and Mark Chater, 'How Did We Get Here?' The Twin

worship in England – the law that the Curriculum and Assessment (Wales) Act 2021 replaces in Wales in relation to religious education. The historical approach shows that the Butler Act was by no means the beginning of the story. Rather, religion and schooling have a long history. Indeed, for most of that history, it was religions themselves that were responsible for education. State involvement in education is a fairly recent phenomenon. Moreover, when the State took an interest in education it supplemented the education activity of churches and then subsidised it. It did not replace it. Even as the twentieth century wore on, the State involvement did not result in the secularisation of the education system. Education does not provide an example of what Charles Taylor has called 'subtraction stories':[2] accounts of things that the historical churches used to do. The overly religious and incredibly localised provisions that still underpin the law on religious education and worship in England are actually twentieth century in origin. The Butler Act was central to this but was also by no means the beginning of the story.

The Butler Act was also not the end of the story. The reforms found in the Education Act 1944 were furthered in the Education Reform Act 1988, which introduced a national curriculum but kept and buttressed the localised regulation of religious education and worship stressing its Christian nature. Ironically it is these later changes that are often seen as being incompatible with the international human rights laws that also developed during the last century and which protect freedom of religion or belief. The current law, then, largely results from compromises made with the churches in the 1940s which were buttressed under the Thatcher Government. This part adopts a chronological approach to explore the non-linear and pragmatic manner in which the law on religion in schools has developed in England.

Narratives' in Mark Chater (ed) *Reforming RE: Power and Knowledge in a Worldviews Curriculum* (John Catt 2020) 21.

2 Charles Taylor, *A Secular Age* (Harvard University Press, 2007) 22.

Chapter 2

THE POSITION BEFORE THE BUTLER ACT

As ever, identifying any starting point in a historical analysis is an arbitrary exercise. As Frederic Maitland put it, 'such is the unity of all history that anyone who endeavours to tell a piece of it must feel that his first sentence tears a seamless web'.[1] This is particularly true when it comes to the history of education. A distinction can be made between the history of formal education, which is a history of state involvement that dates back to the aftermath of the Industrial Revolution, and the wider history of educational experience, a history that dates back to the distant past exploring how children and young adults developed informal training and skills.[2] However, even if the first more narrow approach is taken, the story of formal education actually goes much further back than the Industrial Revolution. This chapter sketches that story.

Primary and secondary education grew out of the work of the churches. Literacy was for centuries tied up with the church.[3] The earliest schools that we know of, dating back to the Anglo-Saxon period, were linked to the church as were the Universities at Oxford and Cambridge, which were established in the early medieval period. However, as Gareth Elwyn Jones and Gordon Wynne Roderick pointed out, 'it is mistaken to regard late medieval education as the province only of the monasteries and the church – there was sufficient demand to foster the creation of grammar schools'.[4] Some of these grammar schools were created independently of the church, sometimes being closely tied with a university or with a borough corporation.

---

1 Frederick Pollock and Frederic W. Maitland, *The History of English Law* (2nd ed, vol 1, Cambridge University Press, 1968 [1898]), 1. For discussion of the need for a historical approach see Russell Sandberg, *Subversive Legal History: A Manifesto for the Future of Legal Education* (Routledge, 2021).
2 Gareth Elwyn Jones and Gordon Wynne Roderick, *A History of Education in Wales* (University of Wales Press, 2003), vii.
3 Ibid., 5.
4 Ibid., 13.

The demand for education gradually grew in the centuries that followed but it remained within the voluntary sector. The churches played a crucial role in this but they did not monopolise it. From the very start, education took various forms: from guilds that were developed in many trades, to dissenting academies that were unofficially set up following the Reformation to Sunday Schools, not to mention later developments that took place under the auspices of the Poor Law.[5] In short, there were a variety of different types of schools. However, schooling was by no means universal. While the wealthy educated their children at home, grammar schools catered for the sons of the middle classes. For the majority, there was no formal education with children typically working alongside their parents in agriculture or factories. There were some attempts to provide for elementary education (often now referred to as primary education). These ranged from 'dame' or 'private venture' schools staffed by women to charity schools founded by the Society for Promoting Christian Knowledge to voluntary day schools established on both faith and non-denominational bases.[6] The motivation for the provision of education 'remained religious, a matter for philanthropy rather than the state'.[7] The bulk of educational provision that had been built up before the nineteenth century, then, 'had been built up by charitable endeavour and private initiative'.[8] By contrast, 'central and local government played no significant role in the running of schools'. Education was something left to what we would today call the voluntary sector.

This changed in the nineteenth century with State involvement deepening throughout the period. Advances were often 'dominated by religious rivalry'. From 1833 grants to support the construction of school buildings were provided but applications had to be channelled through a religious society and had to have at least half the cost raised privately.[9] From 1839, these were supervised by a special Education Committee of the Privy Council which imposed school inspections as a precondition of funding. Government expenditure on education soared from £31,000 in 1841 to £813,000 by 1861 and around four-fifths of that money went to the Church of England. In the 1860s, in addition to building costs, payment was made to schools on

---

5 About three quarters of all working class children were registered in Sunday Schools run by both the Church of England and other churches: William Cornish et al, *Law and Society in England 1750-1950* (2nd ed, Hart, 2019), 420.
6 Ibid., 411.
7 Gareth Elwyn Jones and Gordon Wynne Roderick, *A History of Education in Wales* (University of Wales Press, 2003), 27.
8 William Cornish et al, *Law and Society in England 1750-1950* (2nd ed, Hart, 2019), 411.
9 Ibid., 413–414.

the basis of 4 shillings per child who attended (with 8 shillings more if the child passed certain examinations).[10] Such government funding now made the continued interplay between education and religion more controversial. Some dissenting groups did not seek State aid and by 1815 there were over 350 independent dissenter schools.[11] And the issue of what religion was to be taught in schools and whether parents could withdraw their children from religious instruction arose for the first time.

Nineteenth-Century Cases

The Education Committee resisted the call for Church of England doctrine to be taught in all schools that had State funding but unsuccessfully attempted to impose a conscience clause for parents to withdraw their children from religious instruction. This matter led to litigation in the 1840s.

The case of *Attorney-General v Cullum*[12] concerned a charity deed for the common benefit for a parish which included the provision of school education, but which stipulated that a convenient and sufficient portion of the school hours be set apart for reading the Scripture and that no other religious instruction should be introduced into the school. No mention was made as to the religious creed of the staff of the school. The trustees objected stating that staff should be members of the Church of England and that general religious and moral instruction should be given for an hour at least in every school day. Counsel argued that the trustee's position would limit the benefits of the charity to persons of the Church of England, while the charity was intended for the general benefit of inhabitants of Bury. Counsel for the Attorney General argued that while English law tolerated all religions, it did not place the religion of dissenters on an equal footing with that of the Church of England, and if education was provided for then it must be a religious education and religious education must be according to the principles of the Church of England.

Knight Bruce held that the scheme did 'not provide for religious instruction in the sense in which the expression ought to be understood', that is, 'religious instruction according to the doctrines of the Church of England':

---

10 This was intended to incentivise teachers whose salaries would be dependent upon exam performance but in the short term Government expenditure fell as many failed the tests: Ibid., 421.
11 Ibid., 415.
12 [1842] 62 ER 948.

> If education, of course including religious instruction, is to be provided for, I apprehend it must be according to the doctrines and principles of the English Church. I know no other standard or guide to which the Court can resort.

He held that if education was part of the scheme then 'no other course of religious instruction should be adopted than such as in conformity with the Church of England' and 'the masters, mistresses and teachers must be members of the Church of England'. The parties subsequently agreed to modify the scheme as to education to state that staff should be members of the Church of England and that religious instruction should be given during one hour at least of each school day. Further instruction in the liturgy, catechism and articles of the Church of England would be given to the boys whose parents were in communion with the Church of England, but that any two of the trustees might by writing excuse from attendance in church of any boy whose parents were not in communion with the Church of England. Knight Bruce held that he had no objection to this arrangement.

Re The King's Grammar School, Warwick[13] considered amendments to a scheme setting up a grammar school where the headmaster was required to be a graduate of Oxford or Cambridge and in Holy Orders. The amendments required that religious instruction be given during one hour of every school day and that further instruction in the liturgy, catechism and articles of the Church of England would be given to the boys whose parents were in communion with the church and who did not object to receiving such education. These amendments were introduced by the headmaster contrary to his own views in deference to the direction given in *Attorney-General v Cullum*. Lord Lyndhurst, however, held that the clause be omitted on the basis that because the headmaster is required to be in holy orders then:

> It seems to me to better to leave everything relating to religious instruction to his discretion: I think it much better for the establishment, and much better for religion, to do so than to give any specific direction with respect to it.

This did not mean, however, that conscience clauses allowing parents the right to withdraw their child from religious instruction were not permitted. Rather, 'it seems that conscience clauses became usual in any case where the foundation document did not positively require the teaching of a particular

---

13 [1845] 41 ER 747.

dogma'.[14] This is illustrated by the decision in *Re Ilminster Free School*,[15] which concerned a trust to maintain a school where 'godly learning' was to be observed and where the trustees had the power of approving and removing the school master. A member of the Church of England had always been appointed as school master, but more recently dissenters had been admitted into the school and had not been required to be instructed in the tenets of the Church of England. Moreover, some dissenters had been appointed as trustees. Bruce LJ held that religious instruction must 'according to the language and intention of the instrument, be in conformity with the doctrines of the Church of England'. Given the duties of trustees this meant that 'every trustee ought to be a member of the Church of England'. However, he further noted that:

> 'The sons of Dissenters are very properly admitted to participate in the advantages of the school without having the doctrines of the Anglican Church inculcated on their minds, or being instructed in those doctrines or obliged to attend her services.'

This captured the often contradictory position that resulted from the matter being left exclusively to courts to determine with reference to the school's trust deed against the backdrop of the law at the time which recognised and identified with the Church of England as the church established by law while also increasingly tolerating other religions and the rights of dissenters to opt out. Such matters were also complicated by lack of universal provision and geography, meaning that in practice parents had little choice as to where to send their children to be educated.

The Forster Act

A turning point came with the Elementary Education Act 1870, often known as the Forster Act after William Edward Forster who was responsible for education in Gladstone's Government.[16] The Act established local School Boards in areas where there were insufficient voluntary schools. Their function was to build and manage schools to fill up the gaps in the system provided by the

---

14 William Cornish et al, *Law and Society in England 1750-1950* (2nd ed, Hart, 2019), 418.
15 [1858] 44 ER 1097.
16 See James Murphy, *The Education Act 1870: Text and Commentary* (David & Charles, 1973) and Eric E Rich, *The Education Act 1870: A Study of Public Opinion* (Longmans, 1970).

denominations and charities to ensure that education was provided up to the age of thirteen. The Forster Act, therefore, 'saw a move from state subsidiary of voluntary education to state supplementation of voluntary education'.[17] Much of this additional funding came from a local rate. Provision was not free, except for the very poor. The Act therefore introduced a 'dual' system of elementary schooling: the existing 'voluntary schools were financed though government grants, subscriptions, endowments and school fees; the new board schools could raise additional money though the rates'.[18]

The Forster Act was contentious amongst religious groups:[19] while the Church of England 'wished to preserve and even to extend its grip on education; the Non-conformists fiercely opposed any additional financial support for Church schools'.[20] The question of religious teaching dominated the passage of the Bill through Parliament.[21] Parliamentarians considered whether the Act should require compulsory religious instruction, whether it should 'not be used or directed in favour of or against the distinctive tenets of any religious denomination' and whether there should be a conscience clause allowing a right to withdraw from this.[22] In the end, a compromise was reached by what became known as the 'Cowper-Temple clause' (named after the compromise put forward by Liberal MP William Cowper-Temple) that 'no religious catechism or religious formulary distinctive of any particular denomination' was to be taught in these new schools.[23] This proved contentious with Disraeli criticising the compromise on the basis that there should be 'freedom of religious teaching'.[24] The 'Cowper-Temple clause' limited how denominational religious instruction in the new schools could be but did not mean that schools could not teach their religious ethos. Forster himself noted that the objection to catechisms and formularies rested 'not so much on account of the actual words but because the putting them in the hands of

---

17 William Cornish et al, *Law and Society in England 1750-1950* (2nd ed, Hart, 2019), 422.
18 Gareth Elwyn Jones and Gordon Wynne Roderick, *A History of Education in Wales* (University of Wales Press, 2003), 79.
19 See Eric E Rich, *The Education Act 1870: A Study of Public Opinion* (Longmans, 1970), chapter 3 and James Murphy, *The Education Act 1870: Text and Commentary* (David & Charles, 1973), 54–63.
20 Gareth Elwyn Jones and Gordon Wynne Roderick, *A History of Education in Wales* (University of Wales Press, 2003), 79.
21 William Cornish et al, *Law and Society in England 1750-1950* (2nd ed, Hart, 2019), 422.
22 See the House of Commons discussion at Committee stage: HC Hansard (30 June 1870) columns 1236–1263.
23 Elementary Education Act 1870, section 14(2).
24 HC Hansard (30 June 1870) column 1262.

children appeared to be like claiming those children as belonging to a particular church'.[25]

Further safeguards were provided in the Act, allowing parents to withdraw their children from activities that fell outside the clause such as school prayers and scripture lessons.[26] Section 7 stated that for the new public elementary schools, it would not be a condition that the child attends or does not attend 'any Sunday School or any place of worship'. It would also not be a requirement that 'he shall attend any religious observance or any instruction in religious subjects in the school or elsewhere' and that he may be withdrawn from this observation or instruction by his parent. It was stated that the time or times of religious observance or instruction should 'be either at the beginning or at the end or at the beginning and the end' of the school day so that 'any scholar may be withdrawn by his parent from such observance or instruction without forfeiting any of the other benefits of the school'. Parents could also withdraw their children from attending the 'school on any day exclusively set apart for religious observance by the religious body to which his parent belongs'. Inspectors would not inquire into instruction on religious subjects.

The splits caused by these provisions had a significant political effect and were to be far-reaching. The situation was worsened by the fact that the Act only applied to the new elementary schools which were only built where there was no existing sufficient provision. Existing schools could carry on as they were, teaching according to their faith, and a grace period was provided to allow churches to set up new schools before the new system came into effect.[27] As Anthony Howard noted:

> 'The result, inevitably, was a typically British compromise – or more bluntly, muddle – in which some parents could choose between secular and denominational education while others, mainly in rural villages, had no choice but to send their children to schools in which the dogmas of the Established Church formed a specific part of the curriculum. The seeds for the last great battle fought on behalf of the historical forces of Dissent in Britain had been sown. So firmly were they planted that they defied the successive efforts of Governments of differing political complexions over the next seventy years to uproot them'.[28]

---

25 Quoted in James Murphy, *The Education Act 1870: Text and Commentary* (David & Charles, 1973), 61.
26 Gareth Elwyn Jones and Gordon Wynne Roderick, *A History of Education in Wales* (University of Wales Press, 2003), 79.
27 William Cornish et al, *Law and Society in England 1750-1950* (2nd ed, Hart, 2019), 422.
28 Anthony Howard, *RAB: The Life of R A Butler* (Jonathan Cape, 1987), 111.

Subsequent Developments

Numerous pieces of legislation followed extending education provision. For instance, under the Elementary Education Act 1880 children were required to attend school between the ages of 5 and 10, though local authorities could extend this and make exceptions. Attention then began to be paid to post-elementary education, which had remained exclusively provided for under the voluntary system. When the Bryce Commission in 1895 concluded that the demand for secondary education could not be met through the current system, new Higher Elementary Schools became set up from 1900.[29] However, the funding of such schemes by the School Board was successfully challenged in the courts.[30] This led to the Education Act 1902 which replaced the school boards with Local Education Authorities (LEAs) and empowered them to take steps to supply or aid the supply of education beyond the elementary level. This Act was the most important milestone since the Forster Act.

The passage through Parliament of was to become the 1902 Act witnessed 'a great deal of Nonconformist antagonism'.[31] The Act provided that LEAs would 'maintain and keep efficient all public elementary schools within their area' and this would include schools that were not 'provided' by the LEA as long as certain requirements were met.[32] In the words of Cornish et al, this meant that the Act brought the voluntary schools 'under the control of the LEAs'.[33] These were mainly church schools and mainly associated with the Church of England. Such schools were now supported by local taxation and in return LEAs appointed a third of the managers/governors of the school.[34] This meant that 'in return for a modest surrender of independence they had acquired financial security'.[35] This led to civil disobedience from some dissenters who refused to pay their rates knowing that they would fund Church of England schools.[36]

Several provisions in the Act dealt with religion. These distinguished between those schools which were provided by the LEA and those which were now maintained by the LEA but not provided for by it, such as church schools. The position for schools that were provided by the LEA was laid out

---

29 William Cornish et al, *Law and Society in England 1750-1950* (2nd ed, Hart, 2019), 448.
30 *R v Cockerton* [1901] QB 322.
31 William Cornish et al, *Law and Society in England 1750-1950* (2nd ed, Hart, 2019), 451.
32 Education Act 1902, section 7(1).
33 William Cornish et al, *Law and Society in England 1750-1950* (2nd ed, Hart, 2019), 450. Some funding had previously been provided under the Voluntary Schools Act 1897.
34 Education Act 1902, section 6(2).
35 William Cornish et al, *Law and Society in England 1750-1950* (2nd ed, Hart, 2019), 450.
36 Ibid., 451.

in section 4(1). This stated that 'no pupil, shall, on the grounds of religious belief, be excluded from or placed in an inferior position in any school' provided by the council. It also repeated the ban on catechisms founds in previous legislation but now provided an exception. It stated that:

> 'no catechism or formulary distinctive of any particular religious denomination shall be taught in any school, college or hostel so provided except in cases where the council, at the request of parents of scholars, at such times and under such conditions as the council think desirable, allow any religious instruction to be given in the school, college or hostel otherwise than at the cost of the council: Provided that, in the exercise of this power, no unfair preference shall be shown to any religious denomination'.

Section 4(1) also provided that a council could not in its application of funding 'require that any particular form of religious instruction or worship or any religious catechism or formulary which is distinctive of any particular denomination shall or shall not be taught, used or practiced in any school' that was aided but not provided by the council.

The position of schools that were maintained but not provided by the LEA was laid out in section 7(6). This provided that 'religious instruction in a public elementary school not provided by local authority education' was to be in accordance with the trust deed and was to be under the control of the managers / governors of the school unless the trust deed specified differently.

However, section 4(2) provided a conscience clause allowing withdrawal from religious instruction that applied to any schools 'receiving a grant from, or being maintained by a council' under the Act. This clause was similar to that under the Forster Act, though references to the beginning or end of the school day were omitted and instead it was stated that 'the times for religious worship or any lesson on a religious subject shall be conveniently arranged for the purpose of allowing the withdrawal of any scholar therefrom'.

However, there was a significant disconnect between the letter of the law and the social reality in two respects. First, the nature of Religious Instruction remained undefined. Perhaps this reflected the ubiquity and dominance of Christianity, in general, and the Church of England as the established church, in particular, and so there was simply no need to explain what was meant by religion. However, such an automatic identification of Religious Instruction with Christianity / the Church of England rendered somewhat academic provisions which on their surface seemed to prohibit teaching on denominational lines. Second, in many areas there simply was no choice between schools that were provided by the LEA and those which were not.

Many people had no choice but to attend their local Church of England provided school which, although it was now partly maintained by the LEA, could still teach according to its own tenets.

The 1901 Act was not the last letter on education reform in this period. Further legislation followed, particularly the Education Act 1918 which raised the school leaving age further and removed all fees, but these did not affect the rules applying to religious instruction and worship.

Yet, the messiness of the position underlined a feeling of unfinished business. The two World Wars delayed further developments but also provided a catalyst for clarifying and changing the law underscoring the idea that society had changed. Reform was no easy task, however. As Howard noted, 'for almost a century, education had provided the chief arena in which the various religious denominations had exerted their political muscle'.[37] Toward the end of World War II, the issue of reform was to be championed by Rab Butler. But Rab made a rather inauspicious start to his first meeting with Church leaders when his staff overheard him inquiring 'What is an elementary school?', prompting his Parliamentary Under-Secretary to note in his diaries that the new President of the Board of Education had not even yet grasped the difference between elementary and secondary education.[38] Butler proved, however, to be a quick learner.

---

37 Anthony Howard, *RAB: The Life of R A Butler* (Jonathan Cape, 1987), 111.
38 Ibid., 113.

Chapter 3

THE BUTLER ACT

Rab Butler's biographer, Anthony Howard, referred to the Education Act 1944 as 'the single memorial of which Rab would always remain proudest'.[1] The Act renamed the Board of Education to become the Ministry of Education and differentiated between primary, secondary and further education, making LEAs responsible for ensuring that secondary education would be free and universally provided. It ushered in the tripartite system of education of grammar, secondary modern and technical schools. However, comparatively few technical schools were ever established, so in reality it was a bipartite system that came into existence. The Act also revolutionised both the position of the voluntary church schools that existed alongside the State schools and the teaching of religion in both types of school. Prior to the Act, the ban on teaching by catechism only applied to those schools completely run by local authorities. As Butler himself noted in his autobiography, voluntary schools which were mostly run by the churches, 'gave the religious instruction of the Church to which they belonged, while local authority schools gave religious instruction unconnected with the formulary or beliefs of any particular Church'.[2] Moreover, many areas were what he called 'single-school' areas where the Church of England school was the only school available and 'non-conformists naturally resented sending their children to a school which taught the catechism of the Church of England'.

Yet, Butler's reforms would strengthen rather than weaken the position of the Church of England. It has been noted that under the Butler Act 'the role of Anglicanism within education was not only secured but enlarged'.[3] Butler saw the 1902 Act as having damaged both the Conservative Party and the Church of England, and so the Act that he would be remembered for was 'an attempt to bring Church and state back together and reverse the effects of

---

1 Ibid., 139.
2 Lord Butler, *The Art of the Possible: The Memoirs of Lord Butler* (Revised ed, Penguin, 1973), 98.
3 William Cornish et al, *Law and Society in England 1750-1950* (2nd ed, Hart, 2019), 454.

1870 and 1902 in keeping them apart'.[4] These earlier reforms had left unfinished business and education reform had long been mooted. However, the road to reform was to prove rocky with matters often being outside Butler's control. This chapter tells that story.

The Road to Reform

It was manoeuvres from religious leaders themselves that were to prove influential. In February 1941 leaders of the Church of England and the Free Churches published a joint letter to *The Times* laying out their 'five points' for reform.[5] These were that: 'all children in all schools should receive a Christian education'; 'religious education should be a recognised optional subject in teaching colleges'; 'the statutory restriction that religion should be the first or last lesson in the day should be dropped'; 'religious teaching should be inspected'; and 'all schools should start the day with an act of worship'.[6] These demands were repeated at a session with the new President of the Board of Education on Friday 15 August 1941 which Howard described as 'a pretty formidable example of the Church Militant in action'.[7] They were further repeated in a House of Lords debate in February 1942. Howard noted that these five points did not prove particularly difficult to accept and 'they were, in fact, all included ultimately in the 1944 Education Act'.[8] Yet, they required legislation and it was that which was difficult to obtain at war time.

Indeed, Butler's enthusiasm for action suffered a setback when after relaying his intentions to the Prime Minister, Winston Churchill, he received a reply from the Prime Minister on September 1941 that stated: 'It would be the greatest mistake to raise the 1902 controversy during the War, and I certainly cannot contemplate a new Education Bill.'[9] Butler saw this as being 'quite definitive' but 'decided to disregard what he said and go straight ahead'.[10] The Board of Education's thoughts on reform had been put forward in its confidential memorandum *Education After the War*, commonly known as the Green Book. In terms of religion, the Green Book's solution was to remove the ban

---

4 Ibid., 455.
5 Anthony Howard, *RAB: The Life of R A Butler* (Jonathan Cape, 1987), 113.
6 Michael Barner, *The Making of the 1944 Education Act* (Continuum, 2000), 40.
7 Anthony Howard, *RAB: The Life of R A Butler* (Jonathan Cape, 1987), 113.
8 Ibid., 123.
9 Ibid., 115.
10 Lord Butler, *The Art of the Possible: The Memoirs of Lord Butler* (Revised ed, Penguin, 1973), 96.

on denominational religious instruction in secondary schools.[11] Butler thought that this would have 'led to a head on collision with the Free Churches' and so he worked on his own plans for education reform. In early presentations, however, he did not 'go any further on the religious side than to call for a final settlement of the "Dual System" of provided and non-provided schools'. He later noted that he 'was to spend more time trying to reach the settlement than on anything else'. Yet, Butler was not the only one working on changes to religious education at this time. As he noted in his memoirs, developments by religious leaders were already paving the way to a possible solution:

> An important development that met the wishes of the Non-conformists and of many Anglicans was the 'agreed syllabus'. In Cambridgeshire in 1924 a committee of Anglicans, Free Churchmen and teachers had met and had drawn up a syllabus of religious instruction for use in the county's schools. By 1942 the Cambridgeshire syllabus was in use in over 100 local education authorities. Because of this, many Anglican managers were willing to hand over their schools to the local authorities in return for Christian teachings on these lines.[12]

In meetings with church leaders, Butler seized upon this new potential willingness for LEAs to play a greater role in voluntary schools in return for guarantees about religious teaching. On 5 June 1942, at a meeting with the new Archbishop of Canterbury William Temple and other representatives of the National Society (the Church of England's schools organisation), Butler stressed 'the financial challenge the Church of England would face if it sought to maintain its school system unimpaired' and also 'the scale of the educational disadvantages it would be inflicting upon the children in its care'.[13] Moreover, he presented what 'he had convinced himself was the only possible solution to the problem'.[14] This solution which he said that had 'reached after much patience and experimentation was to make an offer of two alternatives'.[15] The solution was described by Howard as follows:

> The key to it lay in its total absence of compulsion – it threw the burden of decision in to the Churches themselves. The offer of State

---

11 Ibid., 97.
12 Ibid., 100.
13 Anthony Howard, *RAB: The Life of R A Butler* (Jonathan Cape, 1987), 125.
14 Ibid., 126.
15 Lord Butler, *The Art of the Possible: The Memoirs of Lord Butler* (Revised ed, Penguin, 1973), 102.

assistance rested on a choice between two alternatives – a choice left to the recipients to make. If the managers or governors of the school were able and willing to contribute 50 per cent of the necessary costs of required improvements or alterations to school buildings, then they could apply for 'aided' status – in which case the managers or governors would continue to appoint staff and organise religious instruction exactly as before. If, however, that 50 per cent contribution was considered too great a strain on limited resources, then the school could elect to become 'controlled' – which meant, in effect that it was taken over by the relevant Local Education Authority, which would automatically acquire a majority on its board of managers. Even 'controlled' schools, were, however, to be guaranteed religious instruction – though it would be conducted on the basis of a non-denominational 'agreed syllabus'. (Temple was later able to modify this by gaining access twice a week for denominational teachers, whether clergy or others, for those whose parents desired it). [16]

The Butler solution was therefore to create two categories of voluntary schools, voluntary controlled schools and voluntary aided schools with the difference between the two being dictated by control and financing. This built upon the existing category of voluntary schools but crucially brought all schools within the system. It was thought that the non-conformist and most Church of England schools would opt for the voluntary controlled model with the additional funding outweighing the cost of loss of some control while Catholic schools would go for the aided model, retaining further control but at a cost of providing more finance themselves. However, as Butler noted 'difficult negotiations lay ahead'.[17] His initial attempt to secure a commitment in the King's Speech for legislation by the summer of 1943 was 'effectively wrecked' by a letter to *The Times* on 2 November 1942 by the Roman Catholic Cardinal-Archbishop of Westminster Arthur Hinsley.[18] It stated that 'the freedom of conscience of all must be respected' as one of the 'great liberties for which we are fighting'. It pointedly concluded that:

> The Catholic body in this country comes mostly from the workers and from the poorer sections of the community. Therefore our Catholic

---

16 Anthony Howard, *RAB: The Life of R A Butler* (Jonathan Cape, 1987), 126.
17 Lord Butler, The Art of the Possible: The Memoirs of Lord Butler (Revised ed, Penguin, 1973), 102.
18 Anthony Howard, *RAB: The Life of R A Butler* (Jonathan Cape, 1987), 128.

parents have a special claim for fair play, especially from any and every party or group that processes to uphold the just claims of the workers and the rights of minorities.

The result was that the only mention in the King's Speech was a non-committal sentence about 'conversations' taking place about the improvements necessary in education.[19] However, this was enough to allow Butler time to meet with and persuade religious leaders from the Church of England, Catholic and non-Conformist churches. Such dialogue proved fruitful and on 16 July 1943 a White Paper entitled 'Educational Reconstruction' appeared. It noted that 'Education in the future must be a process of gradually widening horizons from the family to the local community, from the community to the nation, and from the nation to the world'.[20] It stated that provision would be made 'for the school day to begin with a corporate act of worship', though a parental right to withdraw would be retained.[21] Howard noted that it was 'striking how comparatively limited a part the discussion of the Church Schools played in it'.[22] It simply referred to 'the necessary amendment to the law to enable the schools provided by the voluntary bodies to play their part in the proposed developments'. Yet, despite this vagueness, 'the Roman Catholics attacked the proposals'.[23] Such attacks proved ineffective, however. The Education Bill was published on 15 December 1943 and its passage 'was one of relatively plain sailing', with the exception of a provision on the salary scale of teachers.[24] As Butler noted:

> Though the Roman Catholic interest never accepted the financial basis laid down for voluntary school building the religious clauses aroused far less acrimony and a much greater sense of responsibility in the House of Commons than past experience had suggested was likely. [25]

---

19 Ibid., 129.
20 Quoted in Gary McCulloch, *Educational Reconstruction: The 1944 Education Act and the Twenty-First Century* (Woburn Press, 1994), 176.
21 Ibid., 27.
22 Anthony Howard, *RAB: The Life of R A Butler* (Jonathan Cape, 1987), 134.
23 Lord Butler, *The Art of the Possible: The Memoirs of Lord Butler* (Revised ed, Penguin, 1973), 107.
24 Anthony Howard, *RAB: The Life of R A Butler* (Jonathan Cape, 1987), 136.
25 Lord Butler, *The Art of the Possible: The Memoirs of Lord Butler* (Revised ed, Penguin, 1973), 120.

That less acrimonious spirit extended to Churchill himself who sent a telegram to Butler congratulating him on adding a 'notable Act to the Statute Book' and saying that he won a 'lasting place in the history of British education'.[26] So, what did the Act actually state?

The Education Act 1944

The Act followed the schema that Butler had set. It provided that LEAs would have the power to establish and maintain primary and secondary schools and that those maintained by the LEA would be known as county schools, and those established otherwise would be known as voluntary schools.[27] Voluntary schools would be further divided into controlled or aided schools.[28] In county schools and voluntary controlled schools the 'secular instruction to be given to the pupils' (including the times at which the school day and term would begin and end) would be under the control of the local education authority and the governors of the school.[29] Section 25 stated that 'the school day in every county school and in every voluntary school shall begin with collective worship on the part of all pupils in attendance at the school, and the arrangements made thereof shall provide for a single act of worship attended by all such pupils unless [...] the school premises are such to make it impractical to assemble them, for that purpose'. It was further stated that 'religious instruction shall be given in every county school and in every voluntary school'. As Gary McCulloch noted, this was 'the first time that these had been made statutory obligations for schools'.[30]

The remainder of section 25 then outlined the parental right to withdraw in a similar manner to the previous legislation. It was not to be required as a condition of any pupil attending any county or voluntary school that 'he shall attend or abstain from attending Sunday School or any place of worship'. If a parent requested that their child 'be wholly or partly excused from attendance at religious worship in the school, or from attendance at religious instruction in the school' or from both then 'until the request is withdrawn, the pupil shall be excused from such attendance accordingly'. Where the child was withdrawn and the parent desired him to receive religious instruction of a different kind during the periods in which he is excused, and arrangements

---

26 Ibid., 124.
27 Education Act 1944, section 9.
28 Section 15.
29 Section 23.
30 Gary McCulloch, *Educational Reconstruction: The 1944 Education Act and the Twenty-First Century* (Woburn Press, 1994), 39.

had been made for him to receive that religious instruction during school hours elsewhere then if 'the pupil cannot with reasonable convenience be sent to another county or voluntary school where religious instruction of the kind described by the parent is provided' then the pupil can be withdrawn from the school for such periods provided that this would 'not interfere with the attendance of the pupil at school on any day except at the beginning of end of the school session on that day'.

Section 26 stated that collective worship in county schools should not be 'distinctive of any particular religious denomination' and that the religious instruction given 'shall be in accordance with an agreed syllabus adopted for the school or for those pupils and shall not include any catechism or formulary that is distinctive of any particular religious denomination'. Section 27 stated that in voluntary controlled schools religious instruction would also be given in accordance with the agreed syllabus unless parents requested that their children receive religious instruction in accordance with the school's trust deed. In that scenario, denominational religious instruction should be provided unless it would be unreasonable to do so but this should be for 'not more than two periods in each week'. Up to one-fifth of the staff could be designated as 'reserved teachers' and be selected or dismissed on grounds of their fitness and competence to give such 'religious instruction as is required to be given'. Under section 28, the religious instruction given at a voluntary aided school was under the control of the managers or governors of the school and was to be in accordance with the school's trust deed or where provision was not made in the trust deed in accordance with the practice observed in the school. However, arrangements were to be made for religious instruction in accordance with the agreed syllabus adopted by the LEA where this was requested by parents and where pupils cannot 'with reasonable convenience' attend a school where that syllabus is in use and unless there were 'special circumstances' that made it 'unreasonable' for this to be accommodated. At voluntary aided schools, all teachers would only be appointed if the managers or governors were 'satisfied as to that person's fitness and competence to give such religious instruction' and, other than those appointed to give instruction in accordance with an agreed syllabus, all teachers can be dismissed for failing to give religious instruction 'efficiently and suitably'. Section 30 provided that, with the exception of reserved teachers in a voluntary controlled school and all teachers in a voluntary aided school, 'no person shall be disqualified by reason of his religious opinions, or of his attending omitting to attend religious worship, from being a teacher' or 'shall be required to give religious instruction' or suffer a detriment as a result.

Section 29 and Schedule 5 of the Act dealt with the procedure for preparing the agreed syllabus. Section 29 provided that LEAs would have the power to 'constitute a standing authority council on religious education to advise the authority upon matters connected with the religious instruction to be given in accordance with an agreed syllabus and, in particular, as to the methods of teaching, the choice of books, and the provision of lectures for teachers'.[31] Schedule 5 stated that conference would be convened to prepare any agreed syllabus and this would consist of four committees: the first of these was to consist of the representatives of religious denominations that the LEA considered ought to be represented 'having regard to the circumstances of the area'; the second, in England, was a committee of representatives of the Church of England; the third was to be a committee of teachers; and the fourth of representatives of the local authority. It would be 'the duty of the conference to seek unanimous agreement upon a syllabus of religious instruction to be recommended for adoption by the local education authority' or more than one syllabus, where the LEA proposes to have more than one syllabus which can apply for certain pupils. The LEA was to have regard to any unanimous recommendations made to them.[32] These provisions further entrenched the position of the Church of England since it meant that the church had its own committee that had a deciding vote. [33]

The Butler Act made no further comment as to the content of religious instruction or worship. The matter had been raised by an amendment in the House of Lords by the Bishop of Chichester which stated that the religious instruction shall 'be in accordance with the principles of the Christian faith', stating that this would reflect the first of the five points for reform.[34] Lord Selborne responded that stating it was not necessary to explicitly state this because the Act's provisions on the composition of the Standing Authority Council on Religious Education (SACRE), he noted:

> They have to agree unanimously on the syllabus, and that at any rate ensures that it will be a syllabus which the Church of England can accept, and the Church of England is not going to accept a syllabus which is not in accordance with the Christian faith.

This, for Lord Selborne, put the matter 'beyond any doubt'. He stated that 'it is the intention of the Government and of the Bill that the religious instruction

---

31 Such bodies were optional under the Act and there is evidence of similar bodies existing before the Act.
32 Education Act 1944, section 29.
33 William Cornish et al, *Law and Society in England 1750-1950* (2nd ed, Hart, 2019), 454–455.
34 House of Lords Hansard (21 June 1944) volume 132, Column 362.

required to be given shall be Christian instruction, and that the corporate act of worship shall be an act of Christian worship'. His Lordship argued that:

> If we put in an Act of Parliament that a syllabus had to be in accordance with the Christian faith, it is open to any one of His Majesty's subjects to bring before the secular courts of this country whether a particular syllabus is in accordance with the Christian faith or not; and that secular courts deciding such matters would result in 'a good deal of trouble. [...] We might find one learned judge saying this or that was, or was not, in accordance with the Christian religion, and other learned and good people violently disagreeing with him.[35]

The provisions of the Butler Act continue to provide the foundations for the law on this matter in England and the religion provisions are probably the most longstanding provisions of the entire Act. Yet, although they were a key consideration in the development of what was to become the 1944 Act, 'changing the status of the Church schools was never the main aim of Rab's plans'.[36] As Howard noted, it was simply 'a necessary precondition if his reforms were to be nationwide and effective'. Butler in his autobiography noted that 'education progress would not be possible unless the problem of the Church schools could be solved'.[37] But he seemed 30 years on to be concerned that the agreed syllabus system had lowered the standard and the religious literacy of the nation. He commented that:

> In the long run, the perfunctory and uninspired nature of the religious instruction in all too many local authority and controlled schools had begun, in the opinion of people well qualified to judge, to imperil the Christian basis of our society.[38]

It is not clear what the evidence was for this assessment, but it was undoubtedly the case that the question of religion in schools remained controversial and would raise its head again when the issue of education reform came to be revisited.

---

35 Ibid., column 368.
36 Anthony Howard, *RAB: The Life of R A Butler* (Jonathan Cape, 1987), 134.
37 Lord Butler, *The Art of the Possible: The Memoirs of Lord Butler* (Revised ed, Penguin, 1973), 99.
38 Ibid., 125.

Chapter 4

THE POSITION AFTER THE BUTLER ACT

Despite Butler's concern that the teaching of religion in schools had come 'to imperil the Christian basis of our society' in the years after the legislation that took his name had been passed,[1] it remained true that the Butler Act had actually increased and consolidated the place of religion in English schools by providing for daily religious worship and compulsory religious instruction in all schools, subject to a parental opt out. The Butler Act brought the church schools within the system, offering them two forms of voluntary status, and also gave the Church of England and representatives of other religious groups responsibility for the authorship of the religious instruction syllabus that would apply in State maintained schools. All of these provisions endure to this day. There have been, of course, significant other changes in the education sphere, most notably the move from grammar schools to comprehensives (pursuant to a 1965 Labour Government Circular and a process that was never universally completed) and the development of the National Curriculum by the Education Reform Act 1988, but these had no effect on the principles that had been underpinned by the Butler Act. Indeed, thanks to a number of amendments in the House of Lords, the Education Reform Act 1988 actually went further in entrenching the position of Christianity. This chapter examines how this happened and how this has left its mark on the current law.

The explicit entrenching of the position of Christianity was likely a reaction against the findings of the Swann Committee in 1985 which had argued that in a pluralistic, multicultural society, 'a major task in preparing all pupils for life […] must […] be to enhance their understanding of a variety of

---

1 Lord Butler, *The Art of the Possible: The Memoirs of Lord Butler* (Revised ed, Penguin, 1973), 125. For detailed discussion of this see Terrence Copley, *Indoctrination, Education and God* (SPCK, 2005), especially chapter 3.

religious beliefs and practices'.² The conservative backlash to this was manifested in a question tabled in the House of Lords by Baroness Cox asking the Government 'what steps they are taking to ensure that all state schools provide a Christian act of worship and Christian religious education for all children whose parents request them'.³ She argued that 'as a nation, we are in danger of selling our spiritual birthright for a mess of secular pottage'. She quoted with approval Lord Selbourne's discussion during the debate on the 1944 Act on the intention of Parliament being that religious instruction and worship would be Christian, but omitted to mention that he argued against including an explicit mention of Christianity in the law. She noted that a survey by *The Times Educational Supplement* in December 1985 found that only 6 per cent of schools were keeping to the letter of the law mostly 'due to logistical difficulties' or because they had a majority of pupils of other faiths. For Baroness Cox, there was 'no justification of breaking the law by denying the act of Christian worship for all pupils whose parents do not wish to exercise their right to withdraw their children from it'. She argued that:

> What is happening in too many of our schools is not only a failure to comply with the law – though that is serious enough – but also a failure to provide young people with a spiritual experience of worship and with an opportunity to become familiar with some of the most precious expressions of Christian faith which are part of this country's heritage, with the scriptures and with prayers and hymns, which have been the spiritual resource of incalculable value for countless people in times past and present.⁴

For Baroness Cox, this 'dreadful betrayal' was made worse by the fact that agreed syllabuses for religious education were increasingly 'multi-faith syllabuses in which Christianity is treated as just one among many faiths and perhaps not even the predominant subject for study'. She expressed concern that 'some multi-faith syllabuses are so worded as to allow the inclusion of secular and political creeds such as humanism and the militant atheism of Marxism'. While 'some teaching about the other great world religions' could increase understanding and respect, that is 'very different from presenting

---

2 'Education for All: Report of the Inquiry into the Education of Children from Ethnic Minority Groups' (Cmnd 9453, 1985).
3 House of Lords Hansard (February 26 1988) volume 493, column 1453.
4 Ibid., columns 1454–1455.

young people with a position of extreme relativism in which all belief systems are presented as a value-free hotchpotch'.[5]

The Earl of Arran, responding for the Government, stressed the importance attached to religious education and worship and pointed to the 'success of the 1944 Education Act'.[6] He said that the Education Reform Bill would 'strengthen' the existing law 'while giving schools greater flexibility in mounting collective worship'. This mirrored an answer to a question in the House of Lords earlier that month in which Baroness Hooper, the Parliamentary Under-Secretary of State for Education, replied that that the Government 'were fully committed to maintaining the requirement for a daily act of worship'.[7] She added that there was 'overwhelming support [...] for greater flexibility in the riming and organisation of daily collective worship' because 'the design and size of secondary school premises make it more difficult than the authors of the 1944 Act envisaged'.[8] However, this seemed to ignore the fact that the Butler Act already made provision for acts of worship to occur in different places at the same time. Baroness Hooper also asserted that 'the law does not explicitly require the act of worship to be Christian although the authors of the 1944 clearly envisaged it would be'. Both of these amendments found their way into the Education Reform Act 1988, which omitted the reference to the act of worship being at the start of the day but now specified that it was to be Christian worship.

The Education Reform Act 1988

The 1988 Act proved to be a watershed moment in the history of education presenting a raft of reforms including the introduction of the National Curriculum.[9] The focus of the Thatcher Government was not especially upon religious matters. However, the Bishop of London successfully tabled amendments to ensure that, as he saw it, the Bill did not represent a move towards secularism or a move away from traditional Christian values. In the House of Lords debate, he stated that these amendments were based upon five main principles:

---

5 Ibid., column 1456.
6 Ibid., column 1482.
7 House of Lords Hansard (4th February 1988) volume 492, column 1187.
8 Ibid., column 1189.
9 On the Act generally see, e.g., Leslie Bash and David Coulby (eds), *The Education Reform Act: Competition and Control* (Cassell, 1989); Denis Lawton (ed), *The Education Reform Act: Choice and Control* (Hodder & Stoughton, 1989) and Michael Flude and Merril Hammer (eds), *The Education Reform Act 1988: Its Origins and Implications* (Falmer Press, 1990).

We have sought to provide a framework for worship which, first, maintains the tradition of worship as part of the process of education, giving proper place to the Christian religion; secondly, maintains the contribution of the collective act of worship to the establishment of values within the school community; yet, thirdly, does not impose inappropriate forms of worship on certain groups of pupils; fourthly, does not break the school up into communities based on the various faiths of the parents, especially in that it makes some groups feel that they are not really part of the community being educated in the school; and, lastly, is realisable and workable in practical terms of school accommodation and organisation.[10]

The Act as amended by the House of Lords stated that daily collective worship, which could be 'a single act of worship for all pupils or separate acts of worship for pupils in different age groups or different school groups',[11] had in a county school to 'be wholly or mainly of a broadly Christian character' and this would be satisfied 'if it reflects the broad traditions of Christian belief without being distinctive of any particular Christian denomination'.[12] However, every act of collective worship did not need to comply with this provision 'provided that, taking the school term as a whole, most such acts that take place in the school do comply'. Powers were given to the Standing Advisory Council on Religious Education (SACRE) to determine whether it was not appropriate for the rule to 'apply in the case of a county school or in the case of any class of description of pupil's, at such a school'.[13] The nature of this power and its application to worship made nonsense of the body's name given that they were neither advising nor confined to dealing with religious education.

The Act also provided that new national curriculum was to be 'a balanced and broadly based curriculum which promotes the spiritual, moral, cultural, mental and physical development of pupils at the school and society; and prepares such pupils for the opportunities, responsibilities and experiences of adult life'.[14] Yet, despite this reference to spirituality,[15] 'religious education' (rather than 'religious instruction'), though remaining compulsory, was

---

10 House of Lords Hansard, 7th July 1988, Column 434.
11 Education Reform Act 1988, section 6.
12 Section 7.
13 SACRES were now compulsory.
14 Section 1(2).
15 On which see Terence Copley, *Spiritual Development in the State School* (University of Exeter Press, 2002).

placed outside the national curriculum, meaning that its contents could still be determined locally. As the Earl of Arran noted, the existing 'local discretion would be threatened if religious education were a foundation subject, as would the present right of parents to withdraw their children from their subject' and the freedoms allowed to faith schools.[16] Yet, again, the Act went further in terms of the Christian content expected. It specified that the agreed syllabus adopted under Schedule 5 of the 1944 Act 'shall reflect the fact that the religious traditions in Great Britain are in the main Christian whilst taking account of the teaching and practices of the other principal religions represented in Great Britain'.[17] Again, the rationale was to 'reinforce' the Butler Act.[18] However, the 1988 Act went beyond the Butler Act.[19] A guide to the Act published by the National Association of Head Teachers noted that 'religious education and collective worship have undergone significant changes in comparison with the Education Act 1944'.[20] It counselled that these changes were 'more likely to bring pressure on schools to comply more fully with the detailed requirements of the Act' and that this would require head teachers 'to be far more detailed and explicit in writing, recording and presenting their arrangements for RE and collective worship', noting that:

> Some of the requirements are worded in vague language which is open to interpretation. [...] It is easy and perhaps tempting to seek to quibble about such phrases or not to take them too seriously. This very vagueness could create difficulties where groups of parents, governors or local/national politicians seek to 'bring schools into line'. The onus will shift to heads who will be required to demonstrate that they have shown reasonableness and willingness to comply with the law. [...] They could then be called to justify [this] by a much wider group than hitherto, a group whose interest will have been stimulated by the letter and spirit of the Act'. [21]

At the very least, the Act made explicit what had previously been implicit – and what may have been implicit and taken for granted in the 1940s was no

---

16 House of Lords Hansard (February 26 1988) volume 493, column 1483.
17 Education Reform Act 1988, section 8.
18 House of Commons Hansard, 15 December 1987, vol 124, column 439W.
19 For a further analysis see Edwin Cox and Josephine M Cairns, *Reforming Religious Education: The Religious Clauses of the 1988 Education Reform Act* (Kogan Page, 1989).
20 National Association of Head Teachers, *NAHT Guide to the Education Reform Act* (Longman, 1989) para 3.1.
21 Ibid., para 6.1.

longer uncontroversial in Thatcher's Britain. This applied not only to the idea that Christianity in general and the Church of England in particular were the norm but also the notion that local areas were largely mono-creedal. The growth of religious diversity and pluralism rendered quaint the idea that each locality could determine their own unique and distinct religious makeup.

The new provisions did not placate concerns. In 1992, Baroness Cox asked a further question on whether or not the provisions relating to religious education were being fulfilled.[22] In her response, the Minister, Baroness Blatch, noted that there was no requirement for local authorities to review agreed syllabuses that were adopted before September 1988, and that this was what was 'giving rise to some of the anxieties that have been voiced' about the 'fruit cocktail' approach to religion.[23] She stressed that 'Christianity should lie at the heart of religious education':

> 'It is vital that children growing up in this country develop a knowledge of the Christian heritage which has had and continues to have such an impact on our society and values'.

Baroness Blatch, however, stressed that the impetus for the review of syllabuses 'must come locally' and expressed her 'hope that the established church and others will continue to press for positive changes'. Reading these debates from the late 1980s and 1990s back, the language and content often feels as if it came from a century before. The profound social and religious changes that occurred in the post–World War period, especially during and since the 1960s,[24] seem to have resulted in nostalgic longing for the explicit reference to Christianity that was considered unwise during the Parliamentary passage of the Butler Act. The fact that the law was seen not to be followed led Parliamentarians to make the law stricter rather than to explore whether the settlement reached in the 1940s was in step with the social reality half a century later.

Baroness Blatch's insistence that the matter was to do with implementation has cast a shadow. The same wariness about re-opening the issue that existed at the start of the twentieth century also existed at the end of that century. There has been no major legislative change to the law on religious education or worship in England since the Education Reform Act 1988. The Education

---

22 House of Lords Handard, 17 June 1992, volume 538, column 248.
23 Ibid., columns 272–273.
24 As discussed in Russell Sandberg, *Religion, Law and Society* (Cambridge University Press, 2014).

Act 1993 made some minor changes mainly to the composition and functions of SACREs, most notably mandating the review of pre-1988 agreed syllabuses and to requiring a five-yearly review of such syllabuses. Other than that, the matter has been left to soft law and guidance. On 31 January 1994, the Department of Education issued Circular 1/94 'Religious Education and Collective Worship' which stated that: 'a syllabus must be based on both Christianity and the other principal religions represented in this country' but this did not 'mean that all religions have to be taught in equal depth or that all of them have to be taught at each key stage'.[25] The circular continued:

> As a whole and at each key stage, the relative content in the syllabus devoted to Christianity should predominate. [...] In this context, the precise balance between Christianity and other religions should take into account both of the national and the local position. In considering this, account should be taken of the local school population and the wishes of local parents, with a view of minimising the number who might exercise the right of withdrawal from RE lessons. [26]

In terms of religious worship,[27] the circular suggested that since worship was undefined by the statute then it must take its ordinary meaning and so 'must in some sense reflect something special or separate from ordinary school activities and it should be concerned with reverence or veneration paid to a divine being or power'.[28] The reference to 'collective worship', however, meant that it should 'necessarily be of a different character from worship amongst a group with beliefs in common', or 'corporate worship'. It stated that 'collective worship and assembly are distinct activities' and '"taking part" in collective worship implies more than passive attendance'.[29] It stated that the worship should not be distinctive of any particular Christian worship but that 'it is open to a school, to have acts of worship that are wholly of a broadly Christian character, acts of worship that are broadly in the tradition of another religion, and acts of worship which contain elements drawn from a number of different

---

25 Department of Education, Circular 1/94: 'Religious Education and Collective Worship', para 34.
26 Para 35.
27 On which see generally Terence Copley, *Worship, Worries and Winners: Worship in the Secondary School after the 1988 Act* (Church House, 1989) which asserted that 'the 1988 Act brought to the surface again all sorts of anxieties' (ibid., v).
28 Department of Education, Circular 1/94: 'Religious Education and Collective Worship', para 57.
29 Paras 58–59.

faiths' provided that the majority of acts of worship over a term are wholly or mainly of a broadly Christian character.[30] Further, some non-Christian elements can be present without depriving it of its broadly Christian character as long as it does 'contain some elements which relate specifically to the traditions of Christian belief and which accord a special status to Jesus Christ'.[31] The situation, then, was far from clear. This was reflected in the position taken by the courts. In *R v Secretary of State for Education ex parte R and D*,[32] it was held that worship which 'reflected Christian sentiments' complied with the Education Reform Act 1988 even if there 'was nothing in them which was explicitly Christian'. From a legal perspective, such a hodgepodge is lamentable; from the standpoint of head teachers and their teaching staff trying to implement the law, the position is even worse.

Many other non-statutory documents have been subsequently published with the effect that there have been a plethora of documents dealing with this matter that have done little to provide clarity.[33] This is likely the effect of having to nuance an outdated legal framework for which there is no political appetite to revisit. At first, these various statutory documents were developed by a number of non-departmental public bodies set up by the Department of Education. Two model syllabuses were published by the then Schools Curriculum and Assessment Authority in 1994; a National Framework for RE was published by the then Qualifications and Curriculum Authority in 2004; and 'Religious Education in English School' in 2010, a review of RE's non-statutory guidance, was published by the then Qualification and Curriculum Development Agency. Then the Department of Education took back powers to determine the national curriculum from 2010 onwards and produced further non-statutory guidance. 'A Curriculum Framework for Religious Education' was published by the Religious Education Council of England and Wales in 2013 (including a foreword by the then Secretary of State).[34] These documents have gradually expanded the range of religions that can be studied. The 2013 Curriculum Framework referred to the teaching of 'religion and worldviews' as including 'Christianity, other principal religions represented in Britain, smaller religious communities and non-religious worldviews such as humanism'.

---

30 Paras 61–62.
31 Para 63.
32 [1994] ELR 495 at 502.
33 See Alan Brine and Mark Chater, 'How Did We Get Here? The Twin Narratives,' in Mark Chater (ed), *Reforming RE: Power and Knowledge in a Worldviews Curriculum* (John Catt 2020), 21.
34 For details of their work see http://www.religiouseducationcouncil.org.uk.

These non-statutory documents have nuanced the provisions of the Education Reform Act 1988 and have done the best they can do given the restrictions brought in by that Act. The explicit entrenching of Christianity in relation to religious education and worship in schools has constrained the ability of the law to keep up to date with social, political and religious change. We are in a similar position to the position we were in prior to the Butler Act: the legal framework is outmoded but there is a reluctance to reopen old wounds. The result is that English law continues to reflect the position drawn in the Butler Act as 'clarified' by the 1988 Act.

Chapter 5

THE CURRENT LAW

The current domestic law governing religious observance in schools can now be found in the Education Act 1996 and the School Standards and Framework Act 1998.[1] These provisions continue to be broadly the same as the settlement reached in 1944, as amended by the 1988 Act. The distinction between maintained schools that are established by the State (local authorities and their predecessors) and those established by voluntary bodies (largely churches and other religious communities) continues to be pivotal.[2] However, there are now other forms of maintained schools (community schools, foundation schools, community-special schools and foundation-special schools)[3] as well as schools that fall outside the maintained category, not only the longstanding independent schools[4] but also notably the hybrid category of Academies and Free Schools, both of which are technically independent schools but which are funded directly by the government rather than being run by the local authority.[5] The distinction between voluntary aided and voluntary controlled schools

---

1 For wider discussion of the issues see, for example, Myriam Hunter-Henin (ed), *Law, Religious Freedom and Education in Europe* (Routledge, 2012), Peter Cumper and Alison Mawhinney (eds), *Collective Worship and Religious Observance in Schools* (Peter Lang, 2018) and Kyriaki Topidi, *Law and Religious Diversity in Education* (Routledge, 2020).
2 School Standards and Framework Act 1998, section 20.
3 Foundation schools are largely State established schools – these may acquire a formal relationship with a charitable trust and become known as 'trust schools', but this category also contains a significant number of voluntarily established schools which, like voluntary schools, already have trust arrangements in place. Community schools, community special schools and foundation special schools (the latter two catering for children with special educational needs) are exclusively State-established schools.
4 Independent schools are funded by fees paid by parents and investments (and some have charitable status). They are largely free to run their own affairs, including setting their own curricula and admission policies but need to be registered with the Department for Children, Schools and Families and are subject to inspection either by Ofsted or by an inspectorate approved by the Secretary of State
5 Academies are set up by private or charitable 'sponsors' who are funded fully by central government by means of a funding agreement with the sponsors. All maintained

remains vital with the differences being control and financing. Community- and voluntary-controlled schools are run by the local authority, which employ the staff and set admission criteria. Foundation and voluntary-aided schools are run by their governing body.

All types of school that have been established by religious bodies may be designated as having some form of religious character. Attendance at or abstaining from attending a Sunday school or a place of worship cannot be required as a condition of attending a maintained school.[6] Schools with a religious character can restrict admission on grounds of religion or belief.[7] However, they cannot discriminate on any other ground, such as on grounds of sex or race or ethnicity.[8] This has proved controversial since a watertight distinction cannot often be drawn between race and religion.[9]

The basic distinction is between schools that have not been designated as having a religious character and those that have. The following will survey the current laws that apply to both in relation to religious education (RE) and worship.[10]

Religious Education in Schools without a Religious Character

In maintained schools that have not been designated as having a religious character, the governing body and the head teacher must ensure that RE is given

---

schools, both primary and secondary schools, are able to apply to the Secretary of State to become Academies. Where a school is to be converted into an Academy and has been previously designated as having a particular religious character, then the Academy is to be treated as being designated as an independent school having that religious character (See the Academies Act 2010). Free Schools are run on a not-for-profit basis and can be set up by groups such as charities, community and faith groups. Technically, Free Schools are academies. Free Schools are normally brand-new institutions, whereas academies are usually created by converting existing schools run by local authorities.

6 Education Act 1996, section 398.
7 Equality Act 2010, Schedule 11, para 5.
8 In *The Interim Executive Board of X School v Chief Inspector of Education* [2016] EWHC (Admin) 2813 it was held that segregation in a faith school on grounds of sex constituted discrimination under the Equality Act 2010. The motive for the discrimination was irrelevant.
9 *R (on the application of E) v. JFS Governing Body* [2009] UKSC 15.
10 This excludes independent schools who are under no obligation to follow the National Curriculum and requirements as to RE and collective worship but must meet the Independent School Standards, which provide requirements as to the quality of education provided as well as the spiritual, moral, social and cultural development of pupils.

in accordance with the local agreed syllabus.[11] However, Local Authorities[12] should 'have regard to the general principle that pupils are to be educated in accordance with the wishes of their parents, so far as that is, compatible with the provision of efficient instruction and training and the avoidance of unreasonable public expenditure'.[13] Accordingly, if a parent requests that a pupil 'be wholly or partly excused' from receiving RE, the pupil is to be so excused until the request is withdrawn.[14] A pupil may be withdrawn from the school to receive RE elsewhere if the pupil 'cannot with reasonable convenience' be sent to the school where RE of that kind is provided.[15] A pupil may not be withdrawn unless the Local Authority is satisfied that the arrangements proposed are such as will not interfere with the attendance of the pupil at school on any day except at the beginning or end of a school session.[16] No teacher can be required to give RE nor is he or she to 'receive any less remuneration or be deprived of, or disqualified for, any promotion or other advantage...by reason of the fact that he does or does not give religious education'.[17]

Each local authority must establish its own SACRE, which consists of 'representative groups' and other 'persons co-opted as members of the council by members of the council'.[18] The representative groups required are:

(a) a group of persons to represent such Christian denominations and other religions and denominations of such religions as, in the opinion of the authority, will appropriately reflect the principal religious traditions in the area;
(b) except in the case of an area in Wales, a group of persons to represent the Church of England;
(c) a group of persons to represent such associations representing teachers as, in the opinion of the authority, ought to be represented, having regard to the circumstances of the area; and
(d) a group of persons to represent the authority.[19]

---

11 School Standards and Framework Act 1998, section 69; Schedule 19, para 2(2).
12 Under the Local Education Authorities and Children's Services Authorities (Integration of Functions) (Local and Subordinate Legislation) Order 2010, Local Education Authorities (LEAs) are now known as Local Authorities.
13 Education Act 1996, section 9.
14 School Standards and Framework Act 1998, section 71.
15 Section 71(3).
16 Section 71(4).
17 Section 59(3).
18 Education Act 1996, section 390.
19 Section 390(4).

Those represented under (b) should 'so far as consistent with the efficient discharge of the group's functions, reflect broadly the proportionate strength of that denomination or religion in the area'.[20] Moreover:

> Before appointing a person to represent any religion, denomination or associations as a member of the council, the authority shall take all reasonable steps to assure themselves that he is representative of the religion, denomination or associations in question.[21]

This seems to allow the Local Authority to make a value judgement as to whether someone is genuinely representative of a religious group. It is questionable whether this is human rights compliant.

Each Local Authority is required to adopt an 'agreed syllabus' for RE after receiving the advice of a periodic conference convened for that purpose (an Agreed Syllabus Conference). The membership requirements for the Conference are the same as those for the SACRE.[22] The resulting syllabus 'shall reflect the fact that the religious traditions in Great Britain are in the main Christian whilst taking account of the teaching and practices of the other principal religions represented in Great Britain'.[23] The syllabus may be different for different schools, classes or pupils. Such an agreed syllabus must be non-denominational:

> No agreed syllabus shall provide for religious education to be given to pupils at a school to which this paragraph applies by means of any catechism or formulary which is distinctive of a particular religious denomination (but this is not to be taken as prohibiting provision in such a syllabus for the study of such catechisms or formularies). [24]

No agreed syllabus shall provide for RE to be given to pupils at a school 'by means of any catechism or formulary which is distinctive of a particular religious denomination (but this is not to be taken as prohibiting provision in such a syllabus for the study of such catechisms or formularies)'.[25]

These provisions apply to all those who attend school, even to those between the ages of 16 and 18 for whom school attendance is not compulsory.

---

20 Section 390(6)
21 Section 392(2).
22 Schedule 31.
23 Section 375(3).
24 School Standards and Framework Act 1998, Schedule 19, para 2(5).
25 Schedule 19 to the School Standards and Framework Act 1998.

Religious studies (RS) exists as an optional academic subject for students to sit at the age of 16 and 18 (at GCSE and A Level). All students must study RE but there is no need for pupils who study RS to study RE if the RS teaching fulfils the statutory obligations for RE. The specification for RS is determined by Awarding Organisations (often known as exam boards) but this specification must conform to the Subject Content prescribed by the Secretary of State. In 2016, new GCSE Subject Content was issued for RS which placed greater emphasis upon world religions. This guidance stated that the 'subject content is consistent with the requirements for the statutory provision of religious education in current legislation'. In *R (on the application of Fox) v. Secretary of State for Education*,[26] it was held that this was 'a false and misleading statement of law' since complying with the Subject Content would not necessarily deliver the RE obligations since it might not include the study of non-religious views. This underscored that it is not only the letter of the law that is authoritative in terms of content – attention also needs to be afforded to the guidance. It is unfortunate, therefore, that this guidance is as confusing and opaque as it is, given its need to clarify a clearly outdated legal framework. The law on RE in schools without a religious character reflects a bygone age where it was possible to describe the religious make up of a local area. The legal framework simply does not fit in an age of increased religious diversity and where belief in Christianity has declined. The parental opt out is not only problematic in an age where respect is given to the rights of children but also worrying in that it can be used to stop children learning about other faiths, other perspectives, other traditions and other views.

Religious Education in Schools with a Religious Character

In terms of RE in schools with a religious character (often referred to as faith schools), a distinction is drawn between foundation and voluntary-controlled schools on the one hand and voluntary aided schools on the other hand.

In a foundation or voluntary-controlled school with a religious character, RE must be in accordance with an agreed syllabus adopted for the school or for a class of pupils.[27] However, where parents request that their children receive RE in accordance with the provisions of the trust deed relating to the school or in accordance with the tenets of the religion or religious denomination specified in relation to the school, then the governors are under an obligation to 'make arrangements for securing that such RE is given to those

---

26 [2015] EWHC 3404 (Admin).
27 School Standards and Framework Act 1998 Schedule 19 para 3.

pupils in the school during not more than two periods in each week', unless special circumstances render it unreasonable for them to do so.[28]

In voluntary-aided schools with a religious character, RE must be in accordance with the trust deed or with the tenets of the religion or religious denomination specified in relation to the school.[29] However, where parents request that their children receive RE in accordance with any agreed syllabus, and it is not reasonably convenient for the parents to send their children to a school in which that syllabus is in use then the governing body is under an obligation to 'make arrangements for religious education in accordance with that syllabus to be given to those pupils in the school' during the times set apart for the giving of RE in the school.[30]

In all faith schools, then, there is a parental opt out. In foundation or voluntary-controlled schools, this opt out is from the locally agreed syllabus towards so that the child can be taught denominational RE. By comparison, it is the reverse direction of travel in voluntary-aided schools. There the default is denominational RE with an opt out that would allow children to be taught RE in accordance with the locally agreed syllabus.

In short, the position still broadly reflects the settlement drawn by the Butler Act. The same is true for the position of teachers. In foundation or voluntary-controlled schools that have a religious character, provided that there are more than two teachers, the teaching staff will include persons (styled 'reserved' teachers) selected for their fitness and competence to give the required RE and are specifically appointed to do so.[31] The number of such 'reserved' teachers must not exceed one-fifth of the total number of teachers including the head teacher.[32] In the case of reserved teachers, preference may be given in connection with the appointment, remuneration or promotion of teachers at the school to persons whose religious opinions are in accordance with that of the school, who attend religious worship in accordance with those tenets, and who give or are willing to give, RE at the school in accordance with those tenets.[33] Regard may be had, in connection with the termination of the employment or engagement of any reserved teacher at the school, to any conduct on his or her part which is incompatible with the precepts, or with the upholding of the tenets, of the specified religion or religious denomination.[34]

---

28 Para 3(3).
29 Para 4.
30 Para 4(3)–(4).
31 School Standards and Framework Act 1998, section 58(2).
32 Section 58(3).
33 Section 60(3), (5)(a).
34 Section 60(3), (5)(b).

In relation to teachers who are not reserved teachers, the same law applies as for teachers in a school that does not have a religious character.[35] In connection with the appointment of the head teacher, where the head teacher is not to be a reserved teacher, 'regard may be had to that person's ability and fitness to preserve and develop the religious character of the school'.[36]

All of the other teachers are governed by the same rules which apply to schools which do not have a religious character; they cannot be required to give RE or suffer a disadvantage as a result of refusing to do so.[37] In voluntary-aided schools which have a religious character, the rules which apply to reserved teachers may be applied to all teachers.[38] The same is true of independent schools with a religious character.[39] However, in academies the rules are akin to those that apply to foundation or voluntary-controlled schools.[40]

The most striking feature of the law on RE in faith schools is that the position varies considerably depending on the type of school. While it is noticeable that the parental opt out again plays a pivotal role, the effect of the opt out varies and is perhaps more significant here. Where the opt out applies in foundation or voluntary-controlled schools with a religious character, then the children are taught denominational RE which can easily become being taught in a religion as opposed to being taught about a religion. And in voluntary-aided schools with a religious character, then this denominational teaching is the default. Although there is a parental opt out, no protection is afforded for the religious freedom of the children. Geographical factors are likely to exacerbate these issues; the choice of which school to attend is again a parental choice but one that might not be completely free. The decision to attend a school with a religious character might have little to do with the faith of the school – it may be the only school that is nearby.

Religious Worship in Schools without a Religious Character

All community, foundation or voluntary schools are required to provide a daily act of collective worship.[41] This need not be at the beginning of the day and separate acts of worship may be provided for pupils in different ages or

---

35 Section 59(2)–(4).
36 Section 60(4).
37 Section 60(2).
38 School Standards and Framework Act 1998 section 60(5).
39 Section 124A.
40 Section 142AA.
41 School Standards and Framework Act 1998, section70.

school groups.[42] Although normally such worship will take place on school premises, if the governing body is of the opinion that it is desirable for worship on a special occasion to take place elsewhere than on the school premises, it may make arrangements after consultation with the head teacher.[43] Parents have a right to withdraw their children, and sixth formers[44] have a right to withdraw themselves from daily worship.[45] If the parents of a pupil other than a sixth-form pupil requests that their child may be wholly or partly excused from attendance, then that pupil shall be so excused until the request is withdrawn. Likewise, if a sixth-form pupil requests this then they shall be so excused. The same rules that allow pupils withdrawn from RE to exceptionally receive RE elsewhere also apply in relation to pupils withdrawn from religious worship.[46]

Schedule 20 to the School Standards and Framework Act 1998 states that 'the required collective worship shall be wholly or mainly of a broadly Christian character'.[47] Collective worship is of a broadly Christian character 'if it reflects the broad traditions of Christian belief without being distinctive of any particular Christian denomination'.[48] Not every required act of collective worship needs to be of broadly Christian character, 'provided that, taking any school term as a whole, most such acts which take place in the school do comply'.[49]

One of the functions of the SACRE is to advise the Local Authority on 'such matters connected with...religious worship in community schools or in foundation schools'.[50] The SACRE may disapply the requirement in prescribed schools, for particular classes or for descriptions of pupils, that daily worship should mainly be Christian. On the application of the head teacher (after consulting the Governing Body, who should take appropriate steps to consult parents) the SACRE shall 'consider whether it is appropriate for the requirement' to be imposed in 'the case of the school or in the case of any

---

42 Schedule 20, para 2(2)
43 Para 2(6).
44 Those beyond the compulsory age of schooling who are attending the last two years of school.
45 Section 71.
46 Section 71(3).
47 Para 3(2)
48 Para 3(3).
49 Para 3(4).
50 Education Act 1996 section 391.

class or description of pupils at the school'.[51] Similar rights for teachers apply as to worship as to RE.[52]

There is a significant difference between the law on religious worship in theory and in practice, largely because the law on religious worship in schools without a religious character is not only impractical but also reflects a bygone age where religious worship was the norm. References to acts of religious worship are questionable and offensive in a society where many believe in non-religious belief systems or have no faith. The recent extension of the right to opt out to sixth formers not only underlines how archaic the law is (with 18-year olds in schools being expected to have daily acts of worship while their peers in colleges are not) but also poses the question of why the same right to opt out should not be afforded in respect of RE and indeed to younger children who are competent to make their own minds on this matter.

Religious Worship in Schools with a Religious Character

In relation to worship, no distinction is made between foundation, voluntary-aided and voluntary-controlled schools with a religious character. The daily act of collective worship must be in accordance with the trust deed or with the tenets of the religion or religious denomination specified in relation to the school.[53] The same rights to opt out apply as for schools without a religious character.[54]

The law on religion in schools therefore continues as a matter of law to reflect the compromises made in the Butler Act 1944 and the Education Reform Act 1988. Socially and religiously, the law reflects a bygone age where matters could be determined locally (because different localities had a distinct religious makeup), and where the focus could be on the wishes of the parent rather than the religious freedom of the child. The effect of all this is that, according to the letter of the law, there is a lot of religion in schools that are not faith schools: children there are to receive RE that recognises the now questionable 'fact that the religious traditions in Great Britain are in the main Christian' and take part in daily acts of worship that are 'wholly or mainly of a broadly Christian character'. With respect to faith schools, a lot depends upon the type of school but it is possible there for children to be taught only

---

51 Sections 394(1), (5), (6).
52 School Standards and Framework Act 1998, section 59.
53 Schedule 20, para 5.
54 Section 71.

denominational RE and the default is that the daily acts of worship are denominational. The focus on local decision-making with respect to schools without a religious character not only reflects a dated social reality of local areas being largely homogenous in terms of religion but also masks the issue of who the members of SACREs are. The significant religious voice on such SACREs, and the protected position of the Church of England in SACREs in England, is questionable in a society where the historical churches have less social influence than they once did and often hold different views than society at large.

There is an urgent need to revisit and update these domestic education laws. However, they are not the only rules that regulate the place of religion in schools. In addition to guidance at a national and local level, the matter is also increasingly shaped by human rights obligations at an international level. These share the focus on parental choice found in domestic measures but the emphasis on freedom of religion or belief and of equality amongst all religions and belief systems sits uncomfortably and challenges the protection in domestic law of Christianity in general and the particular position of the Church of England, in particular.

Chapter 6

THE HUMAN RIGHTS CONTEXT

Although it is regulated by State law, the law on religious education and worship in England continues to be a local affair. The current legal framework assumes that Christianity is the norm but permits SACREs to make allowances for local variations and gives parents and, in the case of religious worship, sixth-formers the right to withdraw. The law also allows for a variety of different schools with a religious character where, again, the general legal provisions can be altered. However, in a religiously diverse and often sceptical society, many argue that an approach that gives Christianity preferred status is outmoded. It has been observed that collective worship in schools today, if carried out to the letter of the law, demands almost as much commitment from children as from adult members of monastic orders.[1] This is the nub of the problem. Empirical studies have repeatedly reinforced the concerns expressed in the House of Lords by Baroness Cox and others; the current legal framework is simply not being followed by schools.[2] This is especially true of the requirement for a daily act of religious worship. As long ago as 1994, the General Secretary of the Secondary Heads Association stated that:

> A law which cannot be obeyed or enforced is a bad law, and it should be amended. [...] This is undoubtedly the case with regard to collective worship in schools.[3]

---

1 Edwin Cox and Josephine M Cairns, *Reforming Religious Education: The Religious Clauses of the 1988 Education Reform Act* (Kogan, 1989), 42.
2 See, for example, Anna Buchanan, 'The Law on Collective Worship in Welsh Schools – A Critical Study' (Cardiff University: Unpublished LLB Dissertation 2008), discussed in Russell Sandberg and Anna Buchanan, 'Religion, Regionalism and Education in the United Kingdom: Tales from Wales' in Myriam Hunter-Henin (ed) *Law, Religious Freedoms and Education in Europe* (Ashgate, 2012), 107; Peter Cumper and Alison Mawhinney, *Collective Worship in Schools: An Evaluation of Law and Policy in the UK* (AHRC Network Report 2015).
3 Quoted in Peter Cumper, 'School Worship: Praying for Guidance' [1998] *European Human Rights Law Review* 1, 45.

The question of reform has received increased attention in recent years.[4] In 2018, the Commission on RE recommended that RE be renamed Religion and Worldviews, and that a non-statutory programme of study be developed at a national level at a similar level of detail as for History and Geography in the national curriculum.[5] The need to reform the law on religious worship has been singled out in particular. The United Nations Committee on the Right of the Child has expressed its concern that pupils are required by law to take part in religious worship and has recommended that the law be changed to ensure that children themselves, as opposed to their parents, have the right to withdraw.[6] Private Members bills have been repeatedly introduced on the matter but, to date, all have proved unsuccessful.[7]

Many criticisms of the current law have suggested that it is not compliant with human rights and discrimination law standards. However, as with other areas of law, there is a need for caution and nuance in making such assertions.[8] There are two different but equally relevant aspects of the human rights context. The first concerns human rights guarantees about education and specifically the rights of parents. The second concerns human rights guarantees and discrimination law prohibitions concerning freedom of religion or belief. While English laws on religious education and worship meet the first aspect, they arguably fall foul of the second aspect at least in terms of the precise letter of the law.

The Right to Education and the Rights of Parents

In relation to the first aspect, Article 2 of the First Protocol of the European Convention on Human Rights (ECHR) provides that no person shall be denied education, and the State must respect the right of parents to ensure for their children education conforming to the parent's own religious and philosophical convictions. This confers no right to go to any particular school. The

---

4 See, for example, Charles Clarke and Linda Woodhead, *A New Settlement Revised: Religion and Belief in Schools* (Westminster Faith Debates Pamphlet 2018).
5 Commission on Religious Education, *Religion and Worldviews: The Way Forward. A National Plan for RE.* (RE Council, 2018).
6 See, for example, United Nations Committee on the Right of the Child, *Concluding Observations on the Fifth Periodic Report of the United Kingdom of Great Britain and Northern Ireland* (2016).
7 In the 2021-22 Parliamentary session, the Education (Assemblies) Bill passed through the House of Lords but did not secure Government support.
8 Cf. Russell Sandberg and Norman Doe, 'The Strange Death of Blasphemy' (2008) 71(6) *Modern Law Review* 971.

right is infringed only if the claimant is unable to obtain education from the system as a whole.⁹ The United Kingdom has entered a reservation in relation to the second right: the principle affirmed in the second sentence of Article 2 is accepted by the United Kingdom only insofar as it is compatible with the provision of efficient instruction and training and the avoidance of unreasonable public expenditure. It has been suggested that the effect of this 'is to qualify a right that is otherwise drafted without a qualifying subsection'.¹⁰

Strasbourg jurisprudence on Article 2 of the First Protocol indicates that the setting and planning of curricula fall within the competence of States, who enjoy a wide margin of appreciation. However, States are forbidden to pursue an aim of indoctrination.¹¹ The State 'must take care that information or knowledge included in the curriculum is conveyed in an objective, critical and pluralistic manner'.¹² The ban on catechisms and the right for parental opt out ensures that these requirements are met.

Freedom of Thought, Conscience and Religion

In relation to the second aspect, Article 9 of the ECHR protects freedom of thought, conscience and religion and the freedom to manifest religion or belief. Following the Human Rights Act 1998, these rights are now actionable in domestic courts and the Equality Act 2010 forbids discrimination on grounds of religion or belief in relation to employment and the provision of goods and services.¹³ Strasbourg and domestic case law have both underlined that protection extends to non-religious beliefs and have taken a generous if sometimes contradictory approach to the definition of belief.¹⁴ However, courts and tribunals have often found that any disadvantage on grounds of religion or belief was justified. Refusals to allow teachers time off during school hours to attend prayers have been upheld by courts as being consistent

---

9 *Abdul Hakim Ali v Head Teacher and Governors of Lord Grey School* [2006] UKHL 14.
10 Samantha Knights, *Freedom of Religion, Minorities and the Law* (Oxford University Press, 2007) para. 4.27.
11 *Kjeldsen, Busk Madsen and Pedersen v. Denmark* (1979) 1 EHRR 71.
12 *Valsamis v Greece* (1997) 24 EHRR 294.
13 For discussion see Russell Sandberg, *Law and Religion* (Cambridge University Press, 2011) and Mark Hill QC, Russell Sandberg, Norman Doe and Christopher Grout, *Religion and Law in the United Kingdom: Great Britain* (3ʳᵈ ed, Kluwer Law International, The Netherlands 2021).
14 See Russell Sandberg, 'Clarifying the Definition of Religion under English Law: The Need for a Universal Definition?' (2018) 20 *Ecclesiastical Law Journal* 132 and Russell Sandberg, 'Is the National Health Service a Religion?' (2020) 22 *Ecclesiastical Law Journal* 343.

with the ECHR[15] and the law prohibiting religious discrimination.[16] Claims based on proselytism have also been unsuccessful.[17]

However, this does not mean that other more general challenges would fail. The law on religious education and worship, particularly its rhetoric as to Christianity and the locally decided and Church of England dominated membership of SACREs, seems vulnerable to challenge by parents, pupils, teachers and would-be SACRE members who feel that they are constrained from manifesting their beliefs. Courts have held that marriage laws that do not enable humanists to manifest their belief are discriminatory and not human rights compliant and similar arguments could be employed in the educational sphere,[18] especially where there is no practical choice of an alternative school and/or a cost to opting out.[19] Indeed, claims have been brought in relation to whether the State is obliged to provide alternative material for those who opt out, though none of these claims have yet reached a contested hearing.[20]

The concerns of the United Nations Committee on the Right of the Child underline that it is questionable whether the fact that the opt out is in the hands of parents rather than children is human rights compliant. The lack of any challenge to date to the fact that there is no opt out for sixth formers even in relation to RE is probably attributable to the likelihood that the letter of the law is not followed in ensuring that sixth formers continue to receive RE. This underscores that the major issue with the current law is that it is not being complied with. While the response to this towards the end of the last century was to 'clarify' the Butler Act requirements through first the Education Reform Act 1988 amendments and then by non-statutory guidance, the question is now whether a new twenty-first century approach is required. That, as the next part will explore, is precisely what Wales has opted for in relation to religious education.

---

15 *Ahmad v Inner London Education Authority* [1978] QB 36.
16 *Mayuuf v Governing Body of Bishop Challoner Catholic Collegiate School & Anor* [2005] Employment Tribunal, Case No. 3202398/04 (21 December 2005).
17 *Powell v Marr Corporation* [2018] UKEAT 1401951/2016.
18 *R (On Application of Harrison) v Secretary of State for Justice* [2020] EWHC 2096 (Admin). See Russell Sandberg, *Religion and Marriage Law: The Need for Reform* (Bristol University Press, 2021).
19 The 'she could have gone to another school' argument put forward in *R (on the application of Begum) v Headteacher and Governors of Denbigh High School* [2006] UKHL 15 have been superseded by the more generous and expansive interpretation of Article 9 ushered in as a result of *Eweida v UK* (2013) 57 EHRR 8. See Russell Sandberg, *Religion, Law and Society* (Cambridge University Press, 2014) 195 *et seq*.
20 *R (on the Application of Harris) v Oxford Diocesan Schools Trust*, Claim No.CO/314/2019.

Part Two

THE NEW WELSH LAW ON RELIGION, VALUES AND ETHICS

In 1999, in the first elections to what was then the Welsh Assembly, the Labour Party won twenty-eight seats and entered into a coalition with the Liberal Democrats who had six seats. One of those six seats was held by Kirsty Williams, who would go on to become the leader of the Welsh Liberal Democrats from 2008 to 2016 with a reputation for championing health and education causes, the key areas in which powers had been devolved to the Welsh Assembly. In the fifth election in 2016, Labour won twenty-nine seats and for the first time since 1999, they again entered into Government with the Liberal Democrats. However, by then the Liberal Democrats only had one seat, which was held by Kirsty Williams. Williams entered the Government as Education Secretary. She then spearheaded the new Curriculum for Wales, building upon the Donaldson Report that had been published in February 2015 and was responsible for the Curriculum and Assessment (Wales) Act 2021, which provides the legislative framework for the new curriculum, including its new approach to religious education. In October 2020, during the passage of the Bill through the Senedd, Williams announced that she would not seek re-election at the 2021 election for what had by now been re-named the Welsh Senedd. In that election, which took place after the Curriculum and Assessment (Wales) Act 2021 had received royal assent, Labour won 30 seats and decided to govern alone. Jeremy Miles was appointed as the new Education Secretary responsible for the implementation of the new curriculum. Although this work is on-going with the implementation of the new curriculum for Wales, the stance of the curriculum and its approach to teaching religion remains very much the legacy of the lone Liberal Democrat.

This part provides a chronological account of how the teaching of religion has been transformed in Wales. It examines in detail how the new Welsh curriculum will radically depart from the status quo in terms of Religious

Education, by renaming it as Religion, Values and Ethics (RVE) and making it a mandatory curriculum requirement, which will fall under the Humanities area of learning with no parental right to opt out in schools without a religious character. This part documents how the new Welsh approach emerged over time and crystallised in the Welsh Government's framing and summaries of consultations, as well as through the Bill's passage through the Senedd. It will reflect on the concerns I raised in consultation responses and submissions, which were cited and discussed in official reports and on the floor of the Senedd.

The following will show how other jurisdictions have much to learn from the radical Welsh approach, especially England where the antiquated law that has been superseded in Wales still applies. However, it will also be suggested that there have been instances where the Welsh Government and Senedd has not been bold enough, especially in relation to schools with a religious character and the continued existence (albeit squeezed) of local decision-making, which sits uncomfortably with the emphasis of the new Welsh curriculum on the autonomous learning journey of each learner and the distinctive and bespoke curriculum that is to be developed by each school. This suggests that, although the Welsh experience should be inspirational, further reform remains needed in Wales and indeed elsewhere.

Chapter 7

THE NEW CURRICULUM FOR WALES

The history of education in Wales has always been at least subtly different to that of England, in part reflecting the different religious makeup of the country (more non-conformist) and other socio-economic differences.[1] For instance, the Welsh Intermediate Act 1889 'resulted in a system of publicly funded secondary education in Wales, thirteen years before England'.[2] There has also never been any equivalent of the Church of England committee on SACREs in Wales, given that the Church of England in Wales was disestablished in 1920.[3] However, most of the uniquely Welsh developments on education were administrative rather than legislative in character.[4] The most up to date instrument on the matter was Circular 10/94, which was published by the former Welsh Office in 1994 and which provided a summary of the current law.

For the most part, laws on education in England applied also in Wales. These often provided an uncomfortable fit with the Welsh social reality and regularly minimised Welsh difference, Welsh culture and perhaps, most notably of all, the Welsh language. The advent of Welsh devolution at the close

---

1 See Gareth Elwyn Jones and Gordon Wynne Roderick, *A History of Education in Wales* (University of Wales Press, 2003) and Gareth Elwyn Jones, *Controls and Conflicts in Welsh Secondary Education 1889-1944* (University of Wales Press, 1982). For a discussion of the values that underpin Welsh legislation, see John Harrington, Barbara Hughes-Moore and Erin Thomas, 'Towards a Welsh Health Law: Devolution, Divergence and Values' (2021), 72 S1 *Northern Ireland Legal Quarterly* 62.
2 Gareth Elwyn Jones and Gordon Wynne Roderick, *A History of Education in Wales* (University of Wales Press, 2003).87.
3 The Welsh Church Act 1914 disestablished the Church of England in Wales and created the Church in Wales. However, certain vestiges of establishment continue to apply to the Church in Wales, meaning that the Church in Wales enjoys some constitutional links with the State. See Norman Doe, *The Law of the Church in Wales* (University of Wales Press, 2002) and Norman Doe (ed), *A New History of the Church in Wales: Governance and Ministry, Theology and Society* (Cambridge University Press, 2020).
4 See Gareth Elwyn Jones, *Which Nation's Schools? Direction and devolution in Welsh Education in the Twentieth Century* (University of Wales Press, 1990).

of the twentieth century provided a turning point, but it took a while for the opportunity provided by the birth to what was then the Welsh Assembly to be grabbed. The Government of Wales Act 1998 created a National Assembly for Wales and a system of executive devolution. This gave the Assembly powers which were generally the same as given to central government ministers in relation to England that were actionable by secondary legislation. The Assembly did not have primary law-making powers. Its executive powers were buttressed by the Government of Wales Act 2006 which, following a successful referendum in 2011 provided a system of legislative devolution initially through passing laws known as Measures. Part 4 of the Government of Wales Act 2006 came into force in 2011, allowing the Assembly to pass primary legislation (now in the form of Acts) in the twenty subject fields in which they have devolved powers. The Senedd and Elections (Wales) Act 2020 empowered the National Assembly of Wales to rename itself as the Senedd Cymru, or Welsh Parliament, which it did with effect from May 2020.

Education has long been one of the areas that have been devolved to Cardiff. The divergence from education policy in England increased during the periods of six different Labour Party Education Ministers in the Welsh Government from 1999 to 2016 with a plethora of initiatives and new developments including the new Foundation Phase, the Welsh Baccalaureate, a different policy on University tuition fees and the creation of an independent exam regulator (Qualifications Wales).[5] Yet, for many years, the Welsh Government confirmed its support for the status quo in terms of religion in schools supporting the Butler Act settlement in terms of different forms of voluntary schools, and the provision of religious education and religious worship in a number of documents.[6] They noted:

> The system [...] consisting of voluntary schools supported by faith organisations and those schools without a religious character, is at the heart of the state school system in Wales. The Welsh Government continues to support the benefits to society that this system brings, both for parental choice and in the interests of raising standards through encouraging constructive diversity. The duality of the system offers learners the

---

[5] For an overall assessment see Gareth Evans, *A Class Apart: Learning the Lessons of Education in Post-Devolution Wales* (Ashley Drake Publishing, 2015) and for one of the Minister's reflections on his time in office see, Leighton Andrews, *Ministering for Education: A Reformer Reports* (Parthian, 2014).

[6] Welsh Assembly Government, *National Exemplar Framework for Religious Education for 3 to 19-Year-Olds in Wales* (2008).

opportunity to be educated within or outside of a faith-based setting in accordance with the wishes of their parents/carers.[7]

Although the Welsh Government has not changed its stance on the matter of schools with a religious character, the introduction of legislative powers enabled greater and more comprehensive changes to occur to the curriculum. In the same way that the changes to religion came about due to the wider educational reforms found in the Butler Act and the Education Reform Act 1988, reform of the law on religious education in Wales was a by-product of wider educational reform to introduce a new curriculum for Wales. This chapter explores the initial moves and thinking behind the new Curriculum for Wales against which the changes in relation to the teaching of religion needs to be placed.

The Curriculum for Wales

The first steps towards a distinctively curriculum for schools in Wales came in March 2014 with the Education Minister, Huw Lewis AM, announcing a new curriculum review to be led by Professor Graham Donaldson, who had previously worked on the Scottish Government's reform programme.[8] The Donaldson Report, *Successful Futures: Independent Review of Curriculum and Assessment Arrangements in Wales*, was published in February 2015 and proposed a radical new curriculum for Wales which would be purpose-based, being 'organised as a continuum of learning from 3 to 16 without phases and key stages', the measurable and bureaucratic preoccupations that had underlined the national curriculum introduced in the late 1980s.[9] The Donaldson Report, noting that 'levels of achievement are not as high as they could and should be',[10] was critical of the current approach on the basis that:

> 'The high degree of prescription and detail in the national curriculum, allied to increasingly powerful accountability mechanisms, has tended to create a culture within which the creative role of the school has become diminished and the professional contribution of the workforce underdeveloped'.[11]

---

7 Ibid., 9.
8 Leighton Andrews, *Ministering for Education: A Reformer Reports* (Parthian, 2014), 263.
9 Graham Donaldson, *Successful Futures: Independent Review of Curriculum and Assessment Arrangements in Wales* (2015), 57.
10 Ibid., 9.
11 Ibid., 10.

In its place, Donaldson proposed a much less restrictive approach that focused on what suited individual learners and which underpinned the autonomy and autonomy of individual schools, teachers and classes. The Report suggested that legislation 'should define a broad set of duties rather than detailed prescription of content'.[12] The curriculum would be organised with three cross-curriculum responsibilities (literacy; numeracy; and digital competence), with four purposes (developing ambitious, capable learners; enterprising creative contributors; ethical informed citizens; and healthy, confident individuals). There would be six Areas of Learning and Experience: Expressive Arts; Health and Well-Being; Humanities; Languages, Literacy and Communication; Mathematics and Numeracy; and Science and Technology.[13]

These Areas of Learning and Experiences (AoLEs) 'should not be seen as watertight compartments but rather a means of organising the intentions for each child and young person's learning';[14] they are 'not timetabling devices'. Donaldson proposed that RE would fit under the Humanities AoLE.[15] The Report noted:

> The Humanities Area of Learning and Experience provides fascinating contexts for children and young people to learn about people, place, time and belief. It will give them an understanding of historical, geographical, political, economic and societal factors and provide opportunities to engage in informed discussions about ethics, beliefs, religion and spirituality.

The Report noted that placing RE within the Humanities area would encourage links to other aspects within the area. It recognised that, although 'RE can and should provide valuable experiences for children and young people that contribute to each of the purposes of education', its position in the curriculum had been 'fragile':

> Its role can be misunderstood as being about the promotion of a particular faith or belief system rather than developing respect and understanding of different forms of religion over time and in different societies.

---

12 Ibid., 101.
13 Ibid., 42, 39.
14 Ibid., 39.
15 Ibid., 46.

The Report concluded that as a result it was 'proposed that RE, and the national expectations for RE, should remain a statutory curriculum requirement'.[16] This was a slightly confusing statement because, as we have seen, the position was that, although RE was compulsory it was not part of the national curriculum and its syllabus was agreed locally not nationally.

The Welsh Government accepted all of the recommendations made by Donaldson and set about developing 'the first ever "made-in-Wales" curriculum'.[17] However, by the time of the publication of the action plan for 2017–21 outlining a 'national mission' to develop a 'transformational new curriculum',[18] Kirsty Williams AM had become Education Minister.

A further development occurred in May 2018 separate to the creation of the new Curriculum for Wales. Kirsty Williams published a letter to Local Authority Directors of Education, which she stated would supersede paragraph 103 of Circular 10/94. That paragraph had stated that the inclusion of representatives of belief systems such as humanism, which do not amount to a religion or religious denomination, on the first Committee within SACREs would be contrary to the law. Williams noted that the appointment of persons to a SACRE is a matter for local authorities and the SACREs, but she also acknowledged the Human Rights Act 1998 which protected freedom of religion or belief. She stated that her legal advice has suggested that representatives from non-religious belief systems may be appointed to such committees. She said that it was the view of the Welsh Government that 'to ensure compatibility with the Human Rights Act 1998 the provisions relating to the constitution of SACREs' were to be interpreted to permit 'the appointment of persons who represent holders of non-religious beliefs in the same way as they permit the appointment of persons who represent holders of religious beliefs'.

However, Williams also gave two provisos to this statement. The first was that 'the non-religious beliefs adhered to by the person to be appointed must be analogous to a religious belief, such as humanism'. The letter stated that:

> 'To be "analogous" we consider the non-religious beliefs must in accordance with case law under the European Convention of Human Rights and the Human Rights Act 1998 attain the necessary level of cogency, seriousness, cohesion and importance to attract protection under the Convention Rights'.

---

16 Ibid., 47.
17 Welsh Government, *Qualified for Life: A Curriculum for Wales – A Curriculum for Life* (2015), 2.
18 Welsh Government, *Education in Wales: Our National Mission – Action Plan 2017-2021* (2017), 42, 2.

The second proviso was that such an appointment would be 'dependent on the relevant local authority's opinion as to whether such a representative would help ensure that the relevant traditions in the local authority's area are appropriately reflected'. She noted that there were 'other areas of contention' within Circular 10/94, that needed to be addressed, but these were raised 'some complex issues' and so 'a review of the guidance will be considered once all information on this matter has been received'.

In the end, the review of the matter came to be superseded by work on the new Curriculum for Wales. Yet, for some time to come, plans for the new curriculum were silent on the matter of religious education. Welsh Government consultations, policies and ultimately legislation on the teaching of religion in schools were only to arrive at the very last moment, perhaps echoing the circumstances that had led to the Butler Act and reflecting the discussions and negotiations that had occurred behind the scenes.

Chapter 8

THE CONSULTATION PHASE

On 28 January 2019, the Welsh Government launched a White Paper to begin the consultation process on 'proposals for legislation on the structure of the new curriculum framework, with the four purposes at its core, the six Areas of Learning and Experiences (AoLEs), the Welsh Language, the English Language, Relationships and Sexuality Education and Religious Education'.[1] In terms of religious education, the document suggested that RE would be part of the Humanities AoLE together with history, geography, social studies and business studies.[2] It stated that RE 'should remain compulsory up to the age of sixteen'.[3] This was different to the current law which requires RE for all those studying in schools beyond the age of 16 years. The document proposed that RE would become optional for sixth formers with schools under an obligation to provide it if it was requested.[4] The document further stated:

> 'It is our intention also that RE reflects our historical and contemporary relationship in Wales to philosophy and religious views, including non-religious beliefs. Therefore the current legislation will be amended to ensure the agreed syllabus for RE takes account of non-religious world views which are analogous to religions (e.g., humanism).'[5]

The White Paper envisaged leaving the position of schools with a religious character largely untouched. It noted that 'Voluntary Aided schools with a religious character will continue to deliver their denominational RE and guidance will be developed by the relevant authorities to make the links with

---

1 Welsh Government, *Our National Mission: A Transformational Curriculum - Proposals for a New Legislative Framework* (2019), para 1.11.
2 Para 2.27.
3 Para 3.29.
4 Para 373.
5 Para 3.66

the Humanities AoLE'.[6] It also suggested retaining but curbing the role of SACREs. As the Paper noted:

> 'Our approach will recognise the local responsibility of the Agreed Syllabus Conferences, local authorities and the place of the denominational syllabus in Voluntary Aided schools but make a clearer connection with a national approach.'[7]

This was to be achieved by stating that 'each Agreed Syllabus Conference and local authority must give due regard to a supporting framework to be produced by Welsh Government'.[8] Furthermore, the membership of the first committee of Agreed Syllabus Conferences and SACREs were to be amended 'to encompass non-religious views that are analogous to religious views' and this was 'to clarify the current legislation and take account of the effect of the Human Rights Act 1998'.[9]

The proposals suggested in relation to schools without a religious character were potentially radical since regarding RE as being compulsory yet also being part of the Humanities AoLE would mark a significant change to the position whereby RE was a separate subject, outside the national curriculum, with its contents prescribed locally. Lessening of the role of SACREs was an obvious consequence of this and the nature of the new Curriculum for Wales generally, but it was telling that abolishing SACREs was not being contemplated.

In committing to retain the status quo on the role of SACREs and in relation to schools with a religious character, the Welsh Government avoided likely difficult battles but also limited how radical their reform could be. This was probably a political decision in order to achieve support or at least stifle opposition to the plans for the new curriculum generally. By retaining these fixtures, changes would now need to be shoe-horned in. By contrast, the Welsh Government indicated that they were open to suggestions regarding the current parental opt out from RE, stating that there was a need to 'determine the appropriate arrangements for this and the similar right to withdraw from sex education in the current system'.[10] The White Paper simply expressed a keenness 'to explore potential approaches to modernise these

---

6 Para 3.69.
7 Para 3.67.
8 Para 3.68.
9 Para 3.71.
10 Para 3.74.

arrangements', ensuring that 'the rights of children and young people are central to considerations but also that full consideration of the impact on all protected characteristics is given', without increasing 'the burden on schools and teachers'.[11] The White Paper welcomed 'views on the case for change and any specific ideas of how to modernise this area'. [12]

This chapter surveys the various consultations on the matter, including the responses to the consultation and the Welsh Government's response. It shows that a new distinctively Welsh approach to religious education quickly developed and was very much shaped by the parameters set in the initial White Paper.

Response to the White Paper

In July 2019, the Welsh Government published the summary of responses to the consultation.[13] The 63.7 per cent of those who responded to the question did not agree with the proposed amendments to RE, with negative responses summarised as saying variously that a clear focus on Christianity was needed, that parental rights should be respected and that RE should not be compulsory.[14] Positive responses suggested the need 'to modernise the content of RE':

> There is potential to explore philosophy and ethics as the route for subject content, potentially an alternative name – as 'RE' fails to encompass all the content (e.g., morality, ethics). Some respondents suggested alternative titles including Religions and Worldviews; Beliefs and Values; Ethics.[15]

A total of 63.1 per cent of respondents agreed with the proposal to make RE optional for sixth formers. A total of 88.7 per cent agreed that the right to withdraw from RE and Relationship and Sexuality Education (RSE) should be retained and it was stressed that 'the European Convention on Human Rights supports the rights of parents'.[16] It was also noted that respondents had suggested that the right to withdraw should be addressed separately for RE and RSE. Those in favour of change indicated that 'if the right to

---

11 Para 3.77.
12 Para 3.78.
13 Welsh Government, *Our National Mission: A Transformational Curriculum - Proposals for a New Legislative Framework – Summary of Response* (July 2019).
14 Ibid., 36.
15 Ibid., 35.
16 Ibid., 39.

withdraw remains schools will encounter challenges to deliver RE in an integrated way'.[17] A total of 90.1 per cent agreed that if the right to withdraw was retained then it should remain with the parents. In terms of alternatives to the right of withdrawal, there were some responses that stated that RE and RSE should be mandatory:

> 'Respondents re-emphasised the need for mandatory RE and RSE. This would ensure learners receive a broad curriculum and are prepared for society; in doing so one of the four purposes for the new curriculum (ethical and informed citizens) is addressed. RE is included in the Humanities AoLE and cross-curricular themes are applied with RE forming part of this delivery'.[18]

It was this minority viewpoint that was to prove influential. Ultimately, the focus of the new curriculum meant that dramatic reform of the teaching of religion would be introduced. Curiously, the Welsh Government considered itself bound more on the questions that they had not consulted on (the position of schools with a religious character and SACREs) than the questions that they had (the reform of religious education in schools without a religious character and the parental opt out). This was clear from the very title of the next consultation document that was produced: the *Consultation on Proposals to Ensure Access to the Full Curriculum for all Learners*. The focus was very much on making RE compulsory and an integral part of the new curriculum.

The Consultation on 'Proposals to Ensure Access to the Full Curriculum for all Learners'

On 3 October 2019, the Welsh Government published a further consultation which made a number of new proposals.[19] It proposed changing the name and content of 'Religious Education' to 'Religions and Worldviews', placing it as a compulsory part of the Humanities area in the new curriculum. The Welsh Government's intention was again said to be that religious education should reflect 'our historical and contemporary relationship in Wales to philosophy and religious views, including non-religious beliefs'.[20] There was therefore a

---

17   Ibid., 41.
18   Ibid., 44.
19   Welsh Government, *Consultation on Proposals to Ensure Access to the Full Curriculum for all Learners* (2019).
20   Para 22.

need to amend current legislation so that 'the agreed syllabus for RE takes account of non-religious world views which are analogous to religions (for example, humanism)'. The paper stated that:

> RE will continue to be compulsory, forming a statutory part of the Humanities Area of Learning and Experience, whilst recognising the local responsibility of the Agreed Syllabus Conferences and local authorities and the place of the denominational syllabus in faith based schools (e.g., Voluntary Aided schools with a religious character). [21]

They also proposed removing the parental right to opt out of such religious education: RE and RSE would be compulsory for all pupils.[22] Although there were 'strong views' on the matter,[23] it was argued that there was 'a strong principle-based case for all school learners to be guaranteed access to RE and RSE'; this was because 'for learners to fully benefit from a broad and balanced curriculum, they must be able to access all parts of the curriculum'.[24] It was further noted that 'the guidance on these subject areas will make it clear that the information covered must be conveyed in an objective, critical and pluralistic manner'[25] and that the Welsh Government would 'ensure that representatives from a variety of communities across Wales, including faith communities, are included and will be able to shape the final guidance'.[26]

The focus of the document on ensuring access to the full curriculum, its human rights-based quiet insistence that 'analogous' non-religious beliefs be explicitly included in both the agreed syllabus and in the formation of the agreed syllabus, its conflation of the opt out in RE and RSE and the highlighting of the new issue of re-naming RE, all shaped how further discussion was to proceed. The focus was not upon the role of SACREs and local authorities, though it could be argued that the new curriculum's focus on individual schools developing their own bespoke curriculum and the Welsh Government's desire for national standards to ensure pluralism would naturally erode the importance of local decision making. The regulation of religious education and worship had been a local matter so that it could take into account the religious makeup of the geographical area in which the school is based. This is a clearly outdated approach given today's pluralistic and

---

21 Para 20.
22 Para 32.
23 Para 33.
24 Para 37.
25 Para 43.
26 Para 44.

multicultural society and the school-based approach of the new curriculum, which raises the question of whether local regulation, discretion and variation are still required. However, it would seem that completely removing that local governance was a step too far for the Welsh Government.

Nevertheless, the consultation quickly generated controversy. The issue of the removal of the parental opt out also proved controversial but more in relation to RSE than RE. However, Humanists UK questioned whether the blanket removal of the right to opt out of religious education would mean that there would be no right to opt out from denominational religious education in schools with a religious character on the basis that teaching may continue to favour particular religions and not include non-religious beliefs.[27] While this was mostly a concern in the case of schools which have a religious character, it was also a concern in relation to schools without a religious character given that under the Education Act 1996 agreed syllabuses 'shall reflect the fact that the religious traditions in Great Britain are in the main Christian'.[28] In a blog post for Law and Religion UK,[29] I suggested that a solution in respect of schools with a religious character could be to distinguish their denominational religious education from the new Religion and Worldviews component of the Humanities AoLE. This would be consistent with the Welsh Government's insistence that there should be no opt out from Religion and Worldviews because it is part of the curriculum. Denominational religious education in schools with a religious character would continue but be outside the curriculum.

However, the main issue of concern – perhaps the main distraction – was the proposed re-naming of RE. This was emphasised by the fact that questions of the consultation explicitly addressed this while assuming the removal of the right to withdraw and other changes would take place. The RE Council responded that the name should be 'Religion and Worldviews' rather than 'Religions and Worldviews' in line with the recommendation of the Commission on RE[30] and to ensure that the subject should include the study of 'religion': they reasoned that reference to religions in the plural suggested a comparative approach that would not include 'a higher-order conceptual

---

27 https://humanism.org.uk/2019/10/03/welsh-government-to-propose-scrapping-the-right-to-withdraw-from-re-in-faith-schools/?
28 Section 375(3).
29 Russell Sandberg, 'Religion in Schools in Wales' (4th October 2019). http://www.lawandreligionuk.com/2019/10/04/religion-in-schools-in-wales/
30 On which see https://www.commissiononre.org.uk/final-report-religion-and-worldviews-the-way-forward-a-national-plan-for-re/

approach' understanding what religion is.³¹ The RE Council suggested that while 'Religions and Worldviews' suggested that 'worldviews' were defined as non-religious worldviews only, by contrast, 'Religion and Worldviews' would suggest that the term 'worldviews' includes religious and non-religious ones. The Catholic Education Service, however, was scathing about the inclusion of non-religious worldviews:

> We are also deeply concerned about the proposed name change of RE to include 'worldviews' as this would represent a dumbing down of RE. By including a range of non-religious 'worldviews' into, what is in Catholic schools, an academically rigorous theological discipline, would water down RE and reduce it to an over-simplistic comparison exercise which fails to understand the deep fundamentals of faith and religion.³²

To me, this criticism was ill-founded. The consultation document empathised that religious education would still recognise 'the place of the denominational syllabus in faith-based schools'.³³ It is difficult to see whether the Catholic objection is to teaching worldviews as part of a comparative religious study or teaching worldviews on an equal playing field. It is only the second option that is objectionable on grounds of religious freedom. In my blog post, I suggested that the real issue was not the name or the inclusion of worldviews but rather that guidance was needed on what would constitute a 'worldview' given that the case law indicated that this was an area of legal uncertainty.³⁴ I argued that adopting a wide and expansive definition would be the best approach here, but the question of where the line is to be drawn was still likely to prove problematic.

Response to the 'Full Curriculum' Consultation

On 21 January 2020, the Welsh Government published the findings of the consultation, announcing that pupils in Wales would have 'universal access'

---

31 https://www.religiouseducationcouncil.org.uk/news/welsh-government-proposal-to-change-the-name-of-re-and-remove-the-right-of-withdrawal/
32 Ibid.
33 Welsh Government, *Consultation on Proposals to Ensure Access to the Full Curriculum for all Learners* (2019) para 20.
34 Russell Sandberg, 'Religion in Schools in Wales' (4ᵗʰ October 2019). http://www.lawandreligionuk.com/2019/10/04/religion-in-schools-in-wales/

to the new Welsh Curriculum from September 2022.[35] The press release stated that the consultation showed support for renaming the subject RE, that the most popular choice was RVE and that the name would be changed when the new curriculum comes into effect. The published analysis of the consultation revealed that 55 per cent were in favour of renaming RE, with 38 per cent against.[36] It was noted that respondents in favour of retaining the name RE 'believed that there is no issue surrounding the name, as it is teaching religion specifically, with other lessons teaching values and ethics' or 'suggested that changing the name would give less time for teaching religion, specifically Christianity'. Indeed, speaking of the consultation process generally, it was noted that:

> 'The suggestions made for changing the name of Religious Education in the new curriculum were not widely supported. The use of the term "ethics" caused confusion for many participants in the consultation.'[37]

Of those who wished to see a name change, 43 per cent respondents suggested 'Religion, Values and Ethics' as opposed to 26 per cent preferring 'Religions and Worldviews' and 31 per cent suggesting one of 151 other possibilities.[38] This meant that the name 'Religion, Values and Ethics' was favoured by 377 respondents while 231 preferred 'Religions and Worldviews' and 606 respondents did not want a name change. Yet, the analysis concluded:

> 'A widespread feeling amongst respondents was that they felt that RE should be renamed Religion, Values and Ethics. Reasons for this included the idea that teaching morals and ethics is important and that the subject should reflect the more expansive focus. In addition, many respondents indicated that worldviews would encourage engagement with a broader range of opinions and beliefs'.

This seemed to suggest that that the term 'values and ethics' was considered to be synonymous with 'worldviews'. Yet, 'Religion, Values and Ethics' is arguably a less focused label than 'Religions and Worldviews' since it does not directly correspond to the understanding of 'religion or belief' as found in international and national human rights and discrimination laws. Perhaps the

---

35   https://gov.wales/children-wales-will-have-universal-access-full-curriculum
36   Wavehill, *Ensuring Access to the Full Curriculum - Consultation Analysis* (2020), 26.
37   Ibid., 6.
38   Ibid., 26.

pluralisation of 'Religions and Worldviews' favoured its rival. Whatever the reason, the choice of name came down to the preference of 146 respondents and became the focus, whereas the real issue was what RVE was going to look like as part of the new Curriculum for Wales and how this was to affect schools with a religious character and the place of local decision-making bodies such as SACREs, who at the very least were also now probably looking at a change of name.

The Publication of Guidance

Further details emerged shortly afterwards after the publication of the consultation response with the publication of guidance on the new curriculum itself.[39] This confirmed that a new Curriculum and Assessment Bill would state that RVE would be one of four mandatory curriculum elements (alongside RSE, Welsh and English) and that RVE would fall under the Humanities area. However, the guidance was confused as to whether this included teaching non-religious worldviews. On the one hand, the 'Statement of What Matters' for Humanities referred to 'various worldviews', 'religious and non-religious beliefs and worldviews' and 'the varied beliefs, values, traditions and ethics that underpin and shape human society', suggesting that RVE was synonymous with Religion and Worldviews and the legal understanding of religion or belief. The 'Designing Your Curriculum' section, however, sometimes just referred just to 'religions' but also spoke of 'religious and non-religious worldviews'. There was also a reference to 'religious and spiritual relationships' under the Health and Well-being AoLE. There was now no reference to non-religious beliefs needing to be 'analogous' to previous ones. It was also notable that the discussion of the Humanities AoLE included more references to the subjects that comprise it than most other areas, with the exception of Expressive Arts, with most other areas being not even split into disciplines. This raised the question of how separate RVE would be.

The RVE Consultation

Further information on RVE in particular was provided in May 2020 with another consultation which strangely took place at the same time as the Curriculum and Assessment Bill's passage through the Senedd, showing how speedy this whole process was. On 5 May 2020, the Welsh Government

---

39 See https://hwb.gov.wales/curriculum-for-wales/

published a consultation specifically on RVE.[40] It stated that the Welsh Government has an 'expectation, based on the current case law' that RVE 'must be pluralistic in nature'.[41] This 'Pluralistic Requirement' meant that RVE 'must be balanced in its content and manner of teaching' and 'should reflect the range of different religions, non-religious philosophical convictions or worldviews'.[42] The consultation put forward two ways in which this could be achieved. The first 'would be to impose a new obligation on all schools to teach RE in a pluralistic manner'.[43] This would 'remove all other restrictions' and 'would also have primacy over any provision set out in their trust deeds'. It is for this reason that the Welsh Government did not favour this option: 'it would have significant implications for schools of religious character and it is not our intention to make fundamental changes to these arrangements'. The Welsh Government favoured the second option, a more nuanced approach which would 'make a number of legislative changes to legislation related to the provision of the agreed syllabus to ensure, so far as a possible, that it meets the Pluralistic Requirement'.[44] Cunningly, although it was presented as the less radical option and as the option that most preserved the autonomy of faith schools, the changes being sought were ground breaking. The first option was presented as a 'straw man' to hide the significance of the changes proposed under the second approach.

Under the second option, the Welsh Government proposed four significant changes:

Requirement to reflect non-religious belief

First, it was proposed to amend existing legislation 'to make it explicit that any agreed syllabus for RVE must reflect both religious beliefs and also non-religious beliefs which are philosophical convictions within the meaning of Article 2 Protocol 1 (and which are therefore beliefs within the meaning of Article 9) of the European Convention on Human Rights'.[45] The Consultation Paper stated that this will 'make it clearer that the philosophical convictions and beliefs that need to be reflected are only those that are caught from time to

---

40 Welsh Government, *Consultation Document – Curriculum for Wales: Religion, Values and Ethics – Legislative Proposals for Religion, Values and Ethics in the Curriculum for Wales Framework* (2020).
41 Para 2.
42 Paras 14, 2.
43 Para 13.
44 Para 14.
45 Para 16.

time by Convention Rights case law and so have a certain level of seriousness, cogency, cohesion and importance under the Human Rights Act 1998'.

This tied in the issue of definition to the case law and again did not include any reference to beliefs needing to be analogous. Crucially, this overstated the clarity of the case law as to the definition of belief under both the ECHR and domestic law. As I noted in my response to the consultation, simply referring to the human rights jurisprudence will not be of any practical help for those designing local syllabi or those planning and teaching lessons in schools. The term 'belief' under human rights law is not limited to philosophical convictions.[46] And a very wide approach has been taken. The European Court of Human Rights has even included political beliefs as being capable of protection.[47] Domestically, where the law is limited to philosophical beliefs, a number of employment tribunal decisions have grappled with the definition of belief with inconsistent results. For example, the same employment tribunal chair decided in two different cases that veganism is capable of being a protected belief but vegetarianism is not.[48]

The Consultation Paper implied that there will be room for interpretation here. It stated that 'beliefs such as humanism or atheism' will be included but that it will be for the Agreed Syllabus Conferences 'to determine what should be included in the agreed syllabus' adding that guidance will be provided. I argued in my response that there was a need to enshrine the pluralistic requirement in legislation. The requirement in current legislation that agreed syllabus must reflect how religious traditions 'are in the main Christian' underscored that without an explicit legislative statement to the contrary a Christian bias and a generally conservative approach would be likely to persist.

Regard to be had to Welsh Government guidance

Traditionally, religious education has been outside the national curriculum with its content decided at local level. However, the consultation document indicated that the direction of travel was clearly away from this in two respects: first from above in the sense that making RVE a mandatory part of the Curriculum for Wales and developing guidance and policy on this pushes

---

46 Though it is for the purpose of discrimination law: Equality Act 2010 section 10.
47 *Hazar, Hazar and Acik v Turkey* (1991), 72 D&R 200; *X v Austria* (1981), 26 D&R 89.
48 *Mr G Conisbee v Crossley Farms Ltd &Ors* [2019] ET 3335357/2018; *Casamitjana v The League of Cruel Sports* [2020] ET 3331129/2018. On which see Frank Cranmer and Russell Sandberg, 'A Critique of the Decision in Conisbee that Vegetarianism is not a Belief' (2020), 22 (1) *Ecclesiastical Law Journal* 36.

power to the Welsh Government from the local level; and second from below in that given the focus in the new Curriculum for Wales is on the particular school and the particular learning experience designing and implementing a bottom–up unique curriculum then this pushes power to individual schools and teachers away from the local level.

This all might suggest that there is no longer any need for SACREs and Agreed Syllabus Conferences or that there is a need at the very least to reduce their powers. However, this was seemingly a step too far for the Welsh Government who were no doubt keen not to antagonise further the religious groups who sit on such groups given how their wider proposals affected schools with a religious character. Instead, the consultation paper proposed significant changes by stealth. In relation to increasing the national regulation of RVE, the paper proposed making a 'new provision requiring the local authority, SACRE and Agreed Syllabus Conference to have regard to guidance issued by the Welsh Ministers in relation to the curriculum in developing and adopting an agreed syllabus'.[49] The shift in power from SACREs to schools was also underlined by the third major change that was proposed.

Schools without a religious character to 'have regard to' rather than 'teach in accordance with' the Agreed Syllabus

Paragraph 20 of the consultation emphasised the grounded nature of the new Curriculum stating that it 'provides a clear national framework within which schools will design a curriculum which meets the needs of their learners', creating 'new duties for schools to design their own curriculum and then implement the curriculum they have designed and adopted'. The document then cleverly used this as the justification to reconsider 'the appropriate status of agreed syllabi'. This allowed the Welsh Government to propose a further major change by stealth. They suggest that 'in general, it will be more appropriate for schools to be required to have regard to an agreed syllabus rather than to teach in accordance with it'. As paragraph 20 concludes: 'This change allows schools some discretion to depart from the Agreed Syllabus'. This is entirely appropriate given the nature of the new Curriculum but it does now question the need for such local bodies to operate.

More importantly, this change could also encourage schools to take an imaginative approach to RVE. Schools would now be able to teach RVE

---

49 Welsh Government, *Consultation Document – Curriculum for Wales: Religion, Values and Ethics – Legislative Proposals for Religion, Values and Ethics in the Curriculum for Wales Framework* (2020) para 19.

as they like provided that they have regard to both the Agreed Syllabus and to Welsh Government Guidance. This is made clearer in paragraph 27 which states that 'in general, we think it is appropriate that schools should be required to have regard to an agreed syllabus, rather than be required to design their curriculum in accordance with an agreed syllabus'. Indeed, the paper clearly placed RVE 'as a mandatory element of their curriculum as part of the Humanities AoLE'.[50] This made it clear that RVE could be taught as part of the Humanities AoLE rather than as a subject in its own right. Having regard to rather than teaching in accordance with the agreed syllabus means that schools will need to teach RVE as part of the school year, but not necessarily as a bespoke lesson that is timetabled weekly or fortnightly. A school which teaches humanities classes that includes some RVE over the course of the year can say that they have regard to the locally agreed syllabus, but would possibly have struggled to say that they taught in accordance with the agreed syllabus. This does raise questions about the right of teachers to refuse to teach RVE: the more diffuse RVE is throughout the curriculum the more difficult it is to insist upon, delineate and enforce this right.

The paper also noted that schools without a religious character would 'continue to be precluded from offering a denominational syllabus'. It further suggested removal of the obligation under Schedule 19 of the School Standards and Framework Act 1998 for secondary schools to provide RE in a different form if the parent wishes. This provision was considered not to fit 'with the principle of seeking to ensure pluralistic RE in schools in Wales'.[51] This is surely correct but, as we will see, this can be compared to what is proposed in relation to schools with a religious character.

Schools with a religious character to provide the option of Pluralistic RVE

The paper embraced the post-Butler Act distinction between voluntary-controlled schools and voluntary-aided schools. It proposed that both voluntary-aided and voluntary-controlled schools with a religious character would be 'required to design their curriculum so that it provides both for two alternatives'.[52] These two alternatives were 'RVE which has been designed in accordance with the trust deeds of the school or the tenets of the faith of the school' and agreed syllabus RVE. Strangely, while for voluntary controlled

---

50 Para 21.
51 Para 22.
52 Paras 24 and 25.

schools, this was termed 'RVE which has been designed having regard to an agreed syllabus', for voluntary aided schools, the text referred to 'RVE which has been designed in accordance with an agreed syllabus'.[53]

In voluntary-controlled schools, the default would be for 'RVE which has been designed having regard to an agreed syllabus but, as now, RVE in line with the trust deeds or tenets of the faith must be provided where a parent requests it'.[54] In voluntary-aided schools, it would be the reverse: 'the default for these schools, as now, will be for learners to receive RVE in line with the trust deeds or tenets of the faith of the school. However, where a parent requests RVE in accordance with an agreed syllabus, it must be provided. The schools will have no discretion as to whether to accept this request'.[55] In other words, the law would basically remain unchanged but all faith schools would need to provide the option of both pluralistic RVE and denominational RVE with a parental right to move from whichever is the default in that particular school to the other. In this respect, the parental opt out got a reprieve of sorts. As I noted at the time,[56] it may be questioned whether it would be better to afford pupils themselves this choice when they come to an age of maturity and whether denominational RVE (that is, taught in the tenets of the faith school) is RVE at all and whether it fulfils the Welsh Government's 'Pluralistic Requirement'. A preferable approach would have been to permit denominational religious education in addition (rather than in place of) pluralistic RVE in schools with a religious character. Requiring faith schools to provide two different forms of RVE on request raised the question of how this is to be resourced and adequately taught.

The consultation analysis summarised the views of the 462 respondents, reporting that a majority (usually around 40 per cent) agreed with each of the recommendations about schools without a religious character, other than the question about whether such schools should have regard to the agreed

---

[53] I noted this at the time in a post on Law and Religion UK (Russell Sandberg, 'Radical Reform of "Religion, Values and Ethics" in Welsh Schools' (6th May 2020). http://www.lawandreligionuk.com/2020/05/06//) but, as we will see, it took a while for the Welsh Government to notice and correct this.

[54] Welsh Government, *Consultation Document- Curriculum for Wales: Religion, Values and Ethics – Legislative Proposals for Religion, Values and Ethics in the Curriculum for Wales Framework* (2020) para 24.

[55] Para 25.

[56] Russell Sandberg, 'Radical Reform of "Religion, Values and Ethics" in Welsh Schools' (6th May 2020). http://www.lawandreligionuk.com/2020/05/06// and in my submission to the consultation.

syllabus to which the majority (45 per cent) were unsure and the question about whether the right for parents to request provision of RVE in line with the tenets of a particular faith should be retained to which 50 per cent disagreed.[57] The majority (64 per cent) of those who responded agreed with the proposals as to voluntary controlled schools but the analysis noted that 'some felt as though the proposals were in contradiction to the broad aims of the legislation, including to promote and embed pluralistic RVE teaching'.[58] The majority (66 per cent), however, disagreed with the proposals on voluntary-aided schools. The analysis quoted my concerns on how the provisions on schools with a religious character, in their words, 'departed from the objective of ensuring universal and plural RVE teaching across Wales'[59] and quoted the Children's Commissioner for Wales as saying that the proposals would 'effectively mean that some children and young people are withdrawn from lessons that are designed to develop their understanding of other faiths and worldviews, or do not get this opportunity at all', and that this 'would therefore restrict access to the curriculum for some and it is not in the best interests of children and young people'.[60] The analysis was published in October 2020 but even by the time in which the consultation closed on 28 July 2020, matters had moved on considerably because the Curriculum and Assessment (Wales) Bill had been published and it had become clear how implementing these proposals would radically reshape the legislative framework on the teaching of religion in schools that had been left unaltered in England and Wales for so long.

---

57   Wavehill, *Curriculum for Wales: Religion, Values and Ethics - Consultation Analysis* (2020), 1, 2.
58   Ibid., 3.
59   Ibid., 25–26.
60   Ibid., 25.

Chapter 9

THE CURRICULUM AND ASSESSMENT (WALES) BILL

On 6 July 2020, the Curriculum and Assessment (Wales) Bill was introduced in the Senedd, together with its explanatory memorandum.[1] Clause 6 of the Bill required schools to teach the six Areas of Learning and Experience (AoLEs), of which Humanities is one, and four mandatory elements (English; Relationships and Sexuality Education; RVE; and Welsh). RVE would also form part of the Humanities AoLE.[2] The main changes in relation to RVE were twofold. First, Schedule 1 stipulated requirements on how RVE would operate in different types of schools. Second, a number of changes were made under Schedule 2 which affects the local authority level, amending existing legislation on agreed syllabuses and advisory councils. This chapter explores these two main changes.

RVE in Schools

Schedule 1 to the Bill made provision for how RVE is to operate and would replace the requirements in Schedule 19 to the School Standards and Framework Act 1998 in Wales (those provisions would now apply only to schools in England, under Schedule 2, para 42). Schedule 1 continued to distinguish between the different types of school following the precedent set by the Butler Act. Maintained schools without a religious character are dealt with by paragraphs 2 and 6, which stated that RVE must be 'designed having regard to the agreed syllabus'.[3] This differs from the School Standards and Framework Act 1998 which states that provision for RE 'must be in accordance with an agreed syllabus adopted for the school or for those pupils'. This

---

1 See https://gov.wales/sites/default/files/publications/2020-07/curriculum-and-assessment-bill-explanatory-memorandum.pdf
2 Explanatory Memorandum, para 3.48.
3 Curriculum and Assessment (Wales) Bill, Schedule 1, para 2(2).

change from 'in accordance' with to 'having regard to' was one of the changes subject to consultation at the time the Bill was introduced. The Explanatory Memorandum stated that schools have the choice whether to deliver RVE as an individual subject or as part of a multidisciplinary or interdisciplinary Humanities approach.[4]

The parental right to opt out found in Schedule 19 to the School Standards and Framework Act 1998 would no longer apply in Wales. Paragraphs 34 and 35 of Schedule 2 provided that the duty to provide religious education under section 69 of the 1998 Act would now only apply in England. Paragraph 36 would amend section 71(1) of the 1998 Act to provide that the parental right to opt out of religious education only applies in England. The right of parents and sixth formers to opt out of religious worship under section 71 (1A–1B) would not be amended. Curiously, neither would be section 71(3) which provides that pupils who have been excused from RE under section 71(1) or religious worship under section 71 (1A–1B) can in certain circumstances be withdrawn from the school for the purpose of receiving religious education. This has a curious effect. The explanatory notes suggested that this means that a pupil withdrawn from religious worship could still receive RE elsewhere under this provision, but that this would be in addition to the RVE that they received at their school.[5] This seemed an odd provision to retain given that the consultation document proposed removing this right (and that other matters subject to consultation were nevertheless assumed in the Bill).

Foundation and voluntary controlled schools that have a religious character are dealt with in paragraphs 3 and 7 of Schedule 1. Again, RVE must be 'designed having regard to the agreed syllabus', but where this does not accord with the provisions of the school's trust deed or religious tenets, then 'the curriculum must also make additional provision for teaching and learning encompassing the mandatory element of RVE that does accord with those provisions or (as the case may be) tenets'.[6] Paragraph 7 provided that a parent could request that their child is provided instead with teaching and learning in accordance with the school's trust deed or religious tenets. This is broadly in line with the current law as found in School Standards and Framework Act 1998 Schedule 19 para 3.

Voluntary-aided schools that have a religious character are dealt with by paragraphs 4 and 8. Here, as under the current law, RVE must accord

---

4 Explanatory Memorandum, para 8.264.
5 Para 187.
6 Curriculum and Assessment (Wales) Bill, Schedule 1, para 3(2), para 3(3)–(4).

with the provisions of the school's trust deed or religious tenets.[7] Schedule 1 further stated that where this does not accord with the agreed syllabus then 'the curriculum must also make additional provision for teaching and learning encompassing the mandatory element of RVE that does accord with the agreed syllabus'.[8] Paragraph 8 provided that a parent can request that their child is provided with this RVE designed in accordance with the agreed syllabus. This is broadly in line with the current law as found in School Standards and Framework Act 1998 Schedule 19 para 4. The language of 'accord' and 'in accordance' with the agreed syllabus used in relation to voluntary aided schools with a religious character remained different to the expression 'having regard to' that applied in relation to other schools. There seemed no logical reason for this disparity.

As I argued at the time,[9] more generally, it could be questioned whether the proposed changes to schools with a religious character facilitate the Welsh Government's vision of universal pluralistic RVE teaching, and therefore run the risk of not being human rights compliant. There is a risk that pupils at these schools will not have access to the pluralistic RVE which the Welsh Government seeks to make universal. I suggested my preferred approach to permit denominational religious education in addition to (rather than in place of) RVE in schools with a religious character.

The Bill also made a significant change in relation to sixth formers. This provision is uniquely dealt within the main body of the Bill under clause 62. RVE was only to be provided for those who request it. This is a change to the current requirement to provide religious education to all registered pupils.[10] This new requirement will be met where 'teaching and learning is provided at the school at a time or times which are convenient for the majority of the pupils who have requested it'.[11] RVE must meet the same requirements for sixth formers as for those of compulsory school age but in this context, these requirements are listed in the Bill itself.[12] The Explanatory Memorandum states that 'A school may make the study of RVE compulsory for all pupils if

---

[7] Para 4(2).
[8] Para 4(3)–(4).
[9] Russell Sandberg, 'Religion, Values and Ethics under the Curriculum and Assessment (Wales) Bill' Law and Religion UK (9th July 2020). https://www.lawandreligionuk.com/2020/07/09/religion-values-and-ethics-under-the-curriculum-and-assessment-wales-bill/ and also in a briefing and written evidence to the Children, Young People and Education Committee.
[10] Explanatory Memorandum, para 3.83.
[11] Curriculum and Assessment (Wales) Bill clause 62(2).
[12] Clause 62(3)–(6).

it wishes. As with pupils under 16, there is no right to withdraw'.[13] However, this is not expressed in clause 62 which talks about RVE being available for those who request it.

RVE and Local Authorities

In terms of agreed syllabuses and advisory councils, the changes under Schedule 2 to the Bill take the form of amendments and repeals to existing legislation. Under paragraph 6 of Schedule 2, section 375 of the Education Act 1996 (which provides for agreed syllabuses for RE) would be amended to state that it only applies to England. Under paragraph 7, a new section 375A would provide for agreed syllabuses for RVE in Wales. These would be determined by each local authority for the use in schools maintained by them, but authorities can make different provisions for different descriptions of schools and different descriptions of pupils. The requirement that the syllabus 'must reflect the fact that the religious traditions in Great Britain are in the main Christian while taking account of the teaching and practices of the other principal religions represented in Great Britain' was retained, but it was also stated that the syllabus 'must also reflect the fact that a range of non-religious philosophical convictions are held in Great Britain'.

The Explanatory Memorandum referred to Kirsty Williams' letter, the Welsh Government circular of May 2018,[14] which laid out the (non-statutory) requirement to include representation from 'non-religious beliefs' provided that they are analogous to religious ones and that this accords with local representation. The Bill by contrast, referred to 'non-religious philosophical convictions' and referred to reflecting such convictions as held in Great Britain rather than the usual principle about reflecting the religious makeup of the area. It also stated that 'the reference to philosophical convictions is to philosophical convictions within the meaning of Article 2 of the First Protocol to the European Convention on Human Rights'. This is where the Bill erred, in my view. As I noted at the time,[15] it was questionable whether citing the ECHR jurisprudence on the definition will give the conceptual clarity needed. The ECHR takes a wide and permissive approach to definition,

---

13 Explanatory Memorandum, para 3.104.
14 Para 3.95.
15 Russell Sandberg, 'Religion, Values and Ethics under the Curriculum and Assessment (Wales) Bill' Law and Religion UK (9th July 2020). https://www.lawandreligionuk.com/2020/07/09/religion-values-and-ethics-under-the-curriculum-and-assessment-wales-bill/ and also in a briefing and written evidence to the Children, Young People and Education Committee.

which does not provide clarity as to where the line is to be drawn in terms of what is being taught. The use of the term 'non-religious philosophical convictions' rather than 'non-religious beliefs' was also strange. The term 'religious and philosophical convictions' is found in Article 2 of the First Protocol of the ECHR on the right to education, while Article 9 talks of freedom of 'religion or belief'. Although Strasbourg institutions have regarded the two phrases to be synonymous, the term 'religion or belief' is used more frequently in domestic law and is easier to understand. It was also questionable whether these provisions would go far enough given the Welsh Government's 'pluralistic requirement'. Retaining the 'in the main Christian' reference is likely to be counter-productive while the reference to the 'range of non-religious philosophical convictions' is vague.

Under paragraph 8, section 390 of the Education Act 1996 would be amended so that SACREs would be renamed Standing Advisory Councils (SACs). The Explanatory Memorandum explains that this is 'because in Wales they will advise on RVE, whilst in England, they will continue to advise on religious education'.[16] This is a welcome name change in that their name has long been inaccurate in that they also deal with religious worship. However, the name change does not recognise that they have also long had powers, which extend beyond being more than advisory. Moreover, as I noted at the time in a briefing and submission to the Children, Young People and Education Committee, given the nature of the new curriculum and the fact that there will be statutory guidance, it is questionable whether there is a need for SACs and locally agreed syllabi at all.

Under paragraph 9, section 390(4) of the Education Act 1996 would be amended so that the list of representative groups on the Standing Advisory Council in Wales would include 'a group of persons to represent such non-religious philosophical convictions ... as, in the opinion of the authority, ought to be represented'. The same definition of 'non-religious philosophical convictions' is to be taken as under the new section 375A. It is stated that this change is 'to ensure compatibility with the Human Rights Act 1998' but that: 'The appointment of such persons is not a mandatory requirement and whether it would be appropriate for so, so as to reflect the local authority area, is a matter for the local authority'.[17] So, the provision enables rather than mandates the representation of groups with non-religious philosophical convictions. This could prove problematic and it is notable that the context

---

16 Explanatory Memorandum, para 27.
17 Para 3.96.

has shifted here from philosophical convictions held in Great Britain to those considered representative by the local authority reflecting the area.

Paragraph 10 would amend section 391 of the Education Act 1996 on the function of advisory councils to include the function of advising the local authority on religious worship in schools without a religious character and RVE. It also, importantly, inserts a new subsection 11 which would state that: 'In exercising its functions under this Act, a council constituted by a local authority in Wales must have regard to any guidance issued by the Welsh Ministers', another one of the changes that was subject to consultation at the time the Bill was published. The Explanatory Memorandum noted that 'responses will inform any potential amendments to existing legislation'.[18]

Other powers would also be transferred to Welsh Ministers. Sections 394–95 of the Education Act 1996 provide that SACREs have the power to deal with applications to disapply the requirement for Christian collective worship. Section 396 gives a power to the Secretary of State to direct a standing advisory council to revoke a determination or discharge a duty in relation to this. Paragraph 13 of the Bill stated that section 396 applies only to England and paragraph 14 would insert a new section 396A that provides a similar power for Welsh Ministers in relation to Wales. Similarly, paragraph 15 would amend section 397 of the 1996 Act in order to clarify that the powers to make regulations in relation to advisory council and agreed syllabus conference meetings and documents now rests with the Welsh Ministers. Paragraph 33 would insert a new section 68A into the School Standards and Framework Act 1998 giving Welsh Ministers with the power to designate schools as having a religious character. This replaces the power given to the secretary of State under section 69(3). Paragraph 37 would make similar provision in relation to independent schools.

Paragraph 26 would make amendments to Schedule 31 of the Education Act 1996 (which deals with convening conferences to agree on a syllabus). These amendments include a duty on local authorities to convene a conference to prepare the first RVE syllabus and also to state that 'a committee of persons representing such non-religious philosophical convictions … as, in the opinion of the authority, ought to be represented'. It also specified the circumstances where in the event of those conditions for adoption not being met, the Welsh Ministers would be required to take action to appoint a body of persons appearing to the Welsh Ministers to possess relevant experience to prepare a syllabus of RVE. Moreover, a new paragraph 14A would be added to the Schedule 31 of the Education Act 1996 to require local authorities,

---

18 Para 4.33.

conferences and a body of persons appointed to prepare a syllabus to have regard to any guidance given by the Welsh Ministers. There is a clear direction of travel here, but perhaps it does not go far enough: if the new Welsh curriculum is the creation of each school, then it may be asked why there is a need to develop a syllabus for RVE at local authority level at all. This question did not arise, however, during the passage of the Bill through the Senedd where the focus remained on other matters.

Chapter 10

THE PASSAGE OF THE BILL

As with all other Bills considered by the Welsh Senedd, the Curriculum and Assessment (Wales) Bill went through four stages. The first is the committee consideration of general principles followed by a plenary debate on general principles. The second is the committee consideration of amendments. The third is the plenary consideration of amendments. The fourth is the passing of the Bill in plenary, followed by Royal Assent unless the Bill is referred to the Supreme Court. This chapter explores the journey of the RVE provisions in the Bill through these four stages. The Curriculum and Assessment (Wales) Bill as a whole enjoyed a relatively smooth passage through the Senedd, led by Kirsty Williams who weathered a number of objections and concerns about aspects of the Bill including notably its provisions on RVE.

Stage 1

Stage 1 of the Bill's passage through the Senedd began on 9th June 2020 and comprised of the consideration of the Bill's general principles by the Children, Young People and Education Committee. They laid their Report on the Bill on 4 December 2020, which supported the change in name of RVE and the removal of the parental right to withdraw, noting that ECHR rights will not be breached if 'in all schools parents can elect for their child to receive objective, critical and pluralistic RVE provision'.[1] It concluded that there were sufficient safeguards in place to ensure this.[2] The report recommended that there was a need to explore whether there should be consistency in language about how all schools take into account the agreed syllabus and whether there should be a right for learners of sufficient maturity to choose the RVE provision they receive where a choice exists.[3] A letter from the minister accepted

---

1 Welsh Parliament Children, *Young People and Education Committee, Curriculum and Assessment (Wales) Bill: Committee Stage 1 Report* (2020), para 558.
2 Para 560.
3 Paras 602–610.

the first point but in relation to the second point stated that under the Bill up until the age of 16 then the parents would make the choice, while post 16 the choice to continue being taught RVE would rest with the pupil. There were three particular points of controversy, however, where the report cited my written evidence and made recommendations to the Welsh Government:

The two syllabus solution for schools with a religious character

The first concern was related to teaching RVE in schools with a religious character, where the Report discussed the concerns about there being more than one syllabus in schools with a religious character. It cited my argument that the agreed syllabus should be available in all schools with denominational RVE being supplementary, noting that Estyn (the Welsh inspections body) and the National Secular Society had made similar points in their submissions.[4] Kirsty Williams was quoted as responding to this concern by recognising that this will have an impact on schools but because 'the number of parents who previously withdrew their child from RVE was negligible our expectation is that this will be mirrored with this proposal'.[5] She added that funding would be made available for the Catholic Education Service and the Church in Wales to 'develop further guidance to support denominational RVE'.

As argued at the time, this response was unconvincing.[6] The number that currently opts out of denominational RE does not affect the point of principle that all Welsh pupils should have non-denominational RVE as the default. Moreover, giving funding to faith groups to support denominational RVE misses the point: if funding is needed then surely it should be for them to develop their non-denominational RVE. And such funding should not be specifically for faith groups given that such RVE is taught in all schools.[7]

---

4 Para 581.
5 Para 596.
6 Russell Sandberg, 'Report on the New Welsh Curriculum and the Teaching of Religion' Sandberg's Subversive Scribblings (4 December 2020). htttp://sandberglaw.wordpress.com/2020/12/04/report-on-the-new-welsh-curriculum-and-the-teaching-of-religion
7 The report also recommended that a framework is provided for the core professional learning, resources and specialist support needed to deliver the necessarily objective, critical and pluralistic teaching of RVE under the New Curriculum: Welsh Parliament Children, *Young People and Education Committee, Curriculum and Assessment (Wales) Bill: Committee Stage 1 Report* (2020), para 648.

The report concluded that 'as a minimum – the ability for parents to require that their child receives agreed syllabus RVE is a necessary safeguard'.[8] But on the potential impact of there being more than one syllabus it concluded that the committee 'remain to be convinced that the practical impact of these provisions will be as significant as feared by some'.[9] The report based this on the fact that some schools in some circumstances are already required to provide more than one type of religious education, that faith groups and schools emphasised that the RE they provided was already objective, pluralistic and critical and that few parents withdrew their children from it. However, these reasons also fail to convince. It is currently rare that there would be more than one type of RE, whereas under the new provisions it could become the norm in schools with a religious character. The report was right to express faith group's concerns that there is no evidence that current RE in schools with a religious character is not objective, pluralistic and critical. But there is also no evidence that it is objective, pluralistic and critical either.

The report considered, however, whether children's rights could be further realised by requiring all schools to provide agreed syllabus RVE, either on its own or supplemented by denominational RVE.[10] It noted that this would raise concerns about breaches of trust deeds, but that it is difficult to come to a view on the issue as the Committee 'are not party to schools' individual trust deeds and cannot be certain what will be included in the agreed syllabi'. Yet, this raises the issue of whether these trust deeds should be examined not least in order to check that they do not infringe the ability to provide pluralistic RVE.

The report also asked the minister in consultation with the Children's Commissioner for Wales to explore further 'the options to further realise children's rights in relation to the Bill's provision for the mandatory element of RVE'.[11] It sought clarification as to why the Bill does not include a right for learners of sufficient maturity to choose the RVE provision they receive where a choice exists.[12] The report highlighted the sufficient attention had not been afforded to the religious freedom of children and recommended that the Welsh Government explore this further in consultation for the Children's Commissioner for Wales.[13] The minister accepted this recommendation.

---

8 Para 600.
9 Para 601.
10 Para 611.
11 Para 612.
12 Para 610.
13 Para 612.

The report also picked up on the inconsistency that voluntary-aided schools were required to design a syllabus that 'accords with' the agreed syllabus while other schools were just required to have 'regard to' it.[14] The report recommended that the Welsh Government clarified during the Stage 1 debate whether there could be consistency between the different types of school in relation to this.[15]

The requirement to reflect that the religious traditions of Great Britain are mainly christian

The second point of concern related to retaining the current legal requirement that teaching in schools should reflect that fact that the religious traditions of Great Britain are mainly Christian. The report quoted suggestions that the reference should be Wales instead before quoting my more general concern that retaining the reference to Christianity was 'likely to encourage both a Christian bias and a conservative approach' and that 'it would be advisable to enshrine the pluralistic requirement in legislation'.[16] Kirsty Williams was then quoted as arguing against a statutory obligation on all schools to reach in a pluralistic manner, because that would 'have significant implications for schools with a religious character' in that it would 'have primacy over any provision set out in their trust deeds'.[17] Further, she noted that the reference to Great Britain was consistent with current provision but that she had asked her officials 'to consider whether this is something that could be revisited for government amendments at Stage 2'.[18] The report recommended that the government 'explore options to amend the Bill to refer to religious traditions and non-religious philosophical traditions in "Wales" as opposed to "Great Britain"'.[19] The minister accepted this recommendation. Though this was welcome, it did not reflect my concern which was not about the words Great Britain but about the reference to Christianity.

The position of SACREs

The third point of concern related to the position on SACREs, with the report citing written evidence that questioned the need for local SACREs and locally

---

14 Para 602.
15 Para 603.
16 Para 592.
17 Para 593.
18 Para 598.
19 Para 613.

agreed syllabi 'given the nature of the new curriculum (which will be created at a school level) and the fact that there will be statutory guidance'.[20] This issue was not raised directly with or commented on by the minister.[21] The report recommended that the Government proceed with its plan to change the title of SACREs but 'that consideration be given to addressing concerns raised by the need to be clear about what Standing Advisory Committees (SACs) exist to advise on' and the balance and fairness of their composition particularly in relation to voting rights. [22]

This recommendation was welcome as far as it went. An argument can be made that SACs should play a minimal role, which further underlines my argument quoted in the Report that consideration should be given of whether there should now be just one Wales-wide SAC. The minister did not accept this recommendation, oddly stating that 'The legislation around SACREs was not part of the Bill' and that 'a review of SACRES including change of name is an issue for a future government'.

Overall, the report gave the green light to the Welsh Government's bold proposals and on 15 December 2020 a debate on the general principles of Bill was held in the Senedd. Various Senedd members spoke about the Bill's provisions on RVE and Kirsty Williams indicated that amendments on that front would be introduced. In her opening speech, the minister said that:

> The amendments I intend to table in Stage 2 will address some of the concerns that have been raised. The Bill will ensure that pluralistic RVE is available to all learners, whilst also ensuring that schools of a religious character can continue to operate in accordance with their trust deeds.[23]

While in her closing speech she said that:

> Members have raised the issue of how, at the moment, schools of a religious character are treated within the legislation. There is a discrepancy that does place extra burdens and I, as I said in my opening remarks, intend to bring forward an amendment that will address that issue.[24]

---

20 Para 624.
21 Para 625.
22 Paras 626 and 627.
23 Senedd Debate, 15 December 2020 at 429.
24 At 544.

However, this was to prove to be a reference to the 'accords with' and/or 'regard to' inconsistency rather than any far-reaching amendment. The fear of trampling over the trust deeds of schools with a religious character seemed to take precedence over the Minister's promise to make pluralistic RVE 'available to all learners'. That could only be achieved if pluralistic RVE was the default in all schools in Wales, including those with a religious character with denominational religious teaching being in addition to rather than instead of pluralistic RVE.

Stage 2

On 16 December 2020 stage 2 began: the consideration of amendments by the Committee. The consideration of the amendments took place on 29 January 2021. Four sets of amendments were discussed regarding RVE. First, the minister tabled amendments that made the language consistent in relation so that all schools must design their RVE syllabus 'having regard to' the locally agreed syllabus rather than ensuring that their syllabus 'accords with' the locally agreed syllabus. This was a sensible amendment and brought all schools in line.

Second, the minister tabled amendments so that the requirement that the RVE syllabus 'must reflect the fact that the religious traditions in Great Britain are in the main Christian' was amended so that the word 'Wales' is used instead of 'Great Britain'. Although this was welcome, it also missed the point that the objection to that phrase is not just about the geography but rather the treatment of Christianity as the norm.

Third, amendments clarified the rules on the composition of SACs stating that a single group of people (rather than two separate groups) need to be appointed to represent 'Christian denominations and other religions and denominations of such religions' and 'non-religious philosophical convictions', and that local authorities must take all reasonable steps to ensure that the number of members appointed 'shall, so far as consistent with the efficient discharge of the group's functions, reflect broadly the proportionate strength of that religion, denomination or non-religious philosophical conviction in the area'. This seemed sensible but the reference to the religious make-up of the locality did seem to hark back to the approach of the current law which we are trying to move away from.

Fourth, Suzy Davies MS (Conservative) tabled a series of amendments which would have the effect that schools with a religious character must design their RVE syllabus with regard to the locally agreed syllabus, *and* the provisions of the school's trust deeds or the tenets of the school. This would have had the effect enacted the proposals that I had suggested. There would be no right for the parent to request alternative RVE teaching but there would be a requirement for schools to 'publicise, or make arrangements to publicise, the procedure for a pupil or their parent to make a complaint about the provisions for teaching and learning' on RVE. The first three groups of amendments were agreed but the amendments tabled by Davies were not agreed.

Stage 3

The Bill then moved onto stage 3, the consideration of amendments in Plenary, which commenced on 1 February 2021 with the Plenary consideration of amendments taking place on the floor of the Senedd on 2 March 2021. While no further government amendments were made in relation to RVE, two amendments were made by Senedd members. Darren Millar MS (Conservative) tabled an amendment that would have reinstated a right of parents to withdraw pupils from RVE while Suzy Davies MS again tabled a series of amendments which would have the effect that schools with a religious character must design their RVE syllabus with regard to the locally agreed syllabus and the provisions of the school's trust deeds or the tenets of the school. Davies' amendment would have achieved the same aim as my suggestion that the locally agreed syllabus RVE should be mandatory in schools with a religious character with denominational RVE being supplementary. They would have ensured that all Welsh learners have access to a pluralistic syllabus informed by non-denominational RVE.

Both of these amendments were defeated on the floor of the Senedd. Suzy Davies MS, introducing the amendments on the teaching of religion, cited a blog post that I had written for Law and Religion UK,[25] and noted my assessment that her amendments were worth considering as they would ensure that all pupils get 'access to a syllabus informed by non-denominational RVE'.[26] The Minister, Kirsty Williams, rejected this amendment on the basis that this requirement might force schools with a religious character to breach their trust deeds. She said that the Welsh Government had no idea what was in the trust deeds and would not legislate in a way that forced schools to breach them:

---

25 Russell Sandberg, 'Why the Religion Provisions in the Curriculum and Assessment (Wales) Bill Need Amending' (25 February 2021). https://lawandreligionuk.com/2021/02/25/why-the-religion-provisions-in-the-curriculum-and-assessment-wales-bill-need-amending/
26 Senedd Debate, 2 March 2021 at 524–525.

The Welsh Government does not see those school trust deeds and so we cannot be certain what they require. As such, we cannot legislate to require schools with a religious character to prepare a single syllabus of RVE which has regard to both an agreed syllabus and the school's trust deeds, as we cannot be certain that it would be possible for the schools to comply with this kind of requirement.[27]

However, this raises the question that if the Welsh Government does not know what is in the trust needs, then how can it be content that the requirements under the Bill as drafted would not breach them. Furthermore, surely this concedes that some learners might not receive pluralistic RVE where the trust deeds are being followed. Williams contended that:

There may be a tension between what a trust deed requires and what the agreed syllabus may require. That tension can be resolved if two RVE syllabuses are designed separately and in accordance with the Bill's current requirements, but the tensions can't necessarily be resolved within a single RVE syllabus.

However, if requiring faith schools to design their RVE syllabus with regard to both their trust deeds and the locally agreed syllabus could potentially breach their trust deeds, then it is difficult to see how the same would not apply to the Bill as drafted which requires faith schools to potentially design two syllabi, one complying with their trust deeds and one with regard to the locally agreed syllabus. The situation under the Bill as drafted whereby some children at a faith school follow a syllabus that exclusively takes regard of the locally agreed syllabus is arguably more likely to breach trust deeds. As Suzy Davies pointed out in her reply, having regard to the locally agreed syllabus would not require a syllabus that has a 50:50 split between denominational and non-denominational RVE. She said that there was a need to define what 'have regard' actually means, and relating it specifically to RVE:

Because having regard doesn't mean that you have to adopt exactly the same amount of each type of curriculum, it doesn't mean that you have to adopt the whole of either of the two types of curriculum that we're talking about here. But what it does mean is that if you decide that part of a curriculum is not to be taught, you have to explain why,

---

27 At 538.

you have to show your workings or what thought you've applied to the decision that you're making.[28]

Williams' other argument against the Davies amendments was that the Church in Wales and Catholic Education Service were in favour of the Bill as currently drafted and had told her that only one child was currently withdrawn from RE, so this meant that the two syllabi requirement would not be overly onerous on faith schools.[29] She added that: 'It is also an option for schools of a religious character to work with neighbouring schools to deliver non-denominational RVE if they wish to do so.'[30] Yet, these practical points did address the question of principle. Moreover, it may be questioned whether the data from the Catholic Education Service actually suggests that the current law is not actually working or if the right to withdraw is too cumbersome and parent focused. It does not provide for the religious freedom of the child – a point that was raised by the Senedd committee report but not discussed further at Plenary.

Notably, Williams now provided caveat to her previous pledge. She now referred to the Bill ensuring 'that all learners will have access to pluralistic RVE where that is wanted'. The final part of the sentence is telling. Learners in schools with a religious character will not necessarily have access to pluralistic RVE – either as a result of parental wish or because in some schools denominational RVE will be the default. It is not even the case that learners will have access to pluralistic RVE where *they* want it, because the choice will be in the hands of parents rather than of the children themselves.

Stage 4

On 9 March 2021, the Senedd approved the Curriculum and Assessment (Wales) Bill and Royal Assent was given on 29 April 2021, the same day as the Senedd was dissolved for the 2021 elections which saw Williams stand down and the Labour Government returned to power with an increase in the number of seats. The Curriculum and Assessment (Wales) Act 2021 is not significantly different to the Bill that had been introduced the previous year, especially in relation to RVE. The next chapter will explore what the new law on teaching religion in schools in Wales now says.

---

28 At 551.
29 At 542.
30 At 541.

Chapter 11

THE NEW LAW

The Curriculum and Assessment (Wales) Act provides the biggest change that schools in Wales will have seen for decades. It will radically transform the curriculum in Wales, ushering in a new pedagogical approach that moves away from a focus on prescribed knowledge to inquiry-based learning which begins with the local experience. It will also transform the teaching of religion. RE will become RVE, with non-religious beliefs included in the content of the subject and in the composition of the local bodies that develop the locally agreed syllabus. The main provisions in the main body of the Act in relation to RVE are section 24 that states that RVE is mandatory for those of school age except for those at nurseries and section 61 which makes RVE optional for those who are above the compulsory school age, placing a requirement on head teachers of maintained schools to provide such RVE for pupils who request it and at times that are convenient for the majority who have requested it. Such RVE 'must reflect the fact that the religious traditions in Wales are mainly Christian, while taking account of the teaching and practices of the other principal Religions represented in Wales, and must also reflect the fact that a range of non-religious philosophical convictions are held in Wales', with 'philosophical convictions' being defined within the meaning of Article 2 of the First Protocol to the European Convention on Human Rights.

As with the original Bill, the main provisions are to be found in Schedules 1 and 2 to the Act. Schedule 1 outlines the design and implementation of RVE. Maintained schools without a religious character must teach RVE which is designed having regard to the locally agreed syllabus.[1] Foundation and voluntary-controlled schools that have a religious character must also teach RVE that is designed having regard to the locally agreed syllabus unless that does not accord with the school's trust deeds or religious tenets in which

---

1 Paras 2 and 6.

case they can make 'additional' provision for this.[2] Although this is styled as being 'additional' in practice it would replace the default provision. The teaching and learning of agreed syllabus RVE does not apply to pupils where the parent of that pupil requests that the teaching and learning is in accordance with the trust deed, etc.[3] The position in voluntary aided schools that have a religious character is the same but the positions of the two forms of RVE are reversed. There, RVE must accord with the school's trust deeds or religious tenets but where that does not accord with the agreed syllabus then the curriculum must make 'additional' provision for RVE that is designed having regard to the locally agreed syllabus.[4] Again, this applies if a parent of a child requests it.

Schedule 2 makes a number of amendments to and repeals of the existing legal framework as it applies to the teaching of religion. Section 375 of the Education Act 1996 dealing with agreed syllabuses now only applies in relation to England.[5] A new section 375A is inserted for Wales which includes the same requirements as to content as found in section 61.[6] Section 390 to Section 392 on SACREs are amended accordingly to provide that in Wales a local authority will constitute a 'standing advisory council on Religion, Values and Ethics' and to explicitly include representatives of 'non-religious philosophical convictions'.[7] A new section 390(6A) and 6B requires that all reasonable steps should be taken to ensure that:

> The number of members appointed to the group to represent a religion, denomination or non-religious philosophical conviction shall, so far as is consistent with the efficient discharge of the group's functions, reflect broadly the proportionate strength of that religion, denomination or non-religious philosophical conviction in the area.

Schedule 31 to the Education Act 1996 is also amended to include a duty to convene the conference to prepare the first syllabus of RVE and to adopt the first syllabus.[8] A new section 14A stipulates that regard must be given to guidance given by the Welsh ministers. The School Standards and Framework Act 1998 is amended to create a new section 68A which gives the Welsh min-

---

2 Para 3.
3 Para 7.
4 Para 4.
5 Schedule 2, para 6.
6 Para 7.
7 Paras 8–11.
8 Para 26.

isters the power to designate schools in Wales as having a religious character, but other than consequential amendments the provisions on the rights of teachers are not amended.[9] Section 69, which provides the duty to provide religious education, now applies only in England.[10] The parental right to opt out found in section 71(1) also now only applies to England.[11] The law on worship is untouched but a new section 71(7A) provides that:

> Regulations made by the Welsh Ministers shall make provision for ensuring that, so far as practicable, every pupil attending a community or foundation special school in Wales attends religious worship unless withdrawn from attendance at such worship—
>
> (a) in the case of a sixth-form pupil, in accordance with the pupil's own wishes, and
> (b) in any other case, in accordance with the wishes of the pupil's parent.

The Curriculum and Assessment (Wales) Act 2021 was not the end of the story, however. Following the appointment of the new Education Minister, Jeremy Miles, attention turned to the implementation of the new curriculum. It was announced that, due to Covid, while the new curriculum would be introduced to all primary school pupils from September 2022 as planned, secondary schools would not be obliged to introduce it until September 2023 when it could be introduced in both of the first two years of secondary school (the original plan had been for it to be introduced in for pupils the first year in September 2022, and then it would follow them through the school so that it applied to the second year of secondary schooling from September 2023). A number of consultation documents were published on the Guidance that would be issued under section 71 of the Act, including one on the Guidance for RVE.[12]

In May 2021, the Welsh Government published draft Guidance on the design and delivery of RVE, which was subject to a consultation period that ended in July. As I noted in my submission to the consultation, some confusion remained in relation to aspects of the Guidance. I identified seven issues where clarity was still needed. In January 2021, the Welsh Government

---

9 Paras 29–33. This includes independent schools under para 37.
10 Paras 34–35.
11 Para 35.
12 Welsh Government, *Consultation Document - Curriculum for Wales Religion, Values and Ethics (RVE) Guidance* (2021).

published its revised guidance. Two new documents were published: a seven thousand word long document on 'Religion, Values and Ethics' was added to the foot of the web page on designing the humanities curriculum;[13] and a further 3,750 words on RVE were also appended to the 'Curriculum for Wales - Summary of Legislation' webpage.[14] For convenience, this chapter will refer to the draft guidance published in May 2021 as the 'Draft Guidance' and will label the two documents published in January 2022 as the 'Curriculum Guidance' and the 'Legislation Summary', respectively.

Although the pieces of guidance published in January 2022 were undoubtedly an improvement on the draft Guidance which was unclear, referred to superseded legal precedents and was generally likely to be of little use to those designing and delivering RVE, many of the seven issues I raised in my response to the consultation remain unaddressed. Not only are parts of the guidance legally questionable, but more importantly the guidance still seems to lack the clarity and relevance needed to be of use to those designing and delivering RVE. This is particularly important given the 'bottom–up' approach of the new curriculum.

The following will discuss the seven issues that I raised in my submission to the original consultation and in a blog post published after the new Guidance was published.[15] It will explore why the Draft Guidance raised these concerns and the extent to which these concerns were resolved in the seemingly finalised Curriculum Guidance and the Legislation Summary.[16]

The Place of RVE within the Humanities AoLE

The Draft Guidance positioned RVE within the Humanities AoLE and underlined that 'each school will need to decide its own approach to curriculum design in the Humanities Area and to how RVE best works within it'. The Curriculum Guidance also makes it plain that RVE is to be understood primarily within the context of the Humanities AoLE. Indeed, this is underlined by its publication in that section of the website. It also states that the

---

13 https://hwb.gov.wales/curriculum-for-wales/humanities/designing-your-curriculum/#religion,-values-and-ethics-guidance
14 https://hwb.gov.wales/curriculum-for-wales/summary-of-legislation/#religion,-values-and-ethics
15 Russell Sandberg, 'Wales: Guidance on Religion, Values and Ethics Published' *Law and Religion UK* (14 January 2022). https://lawandreligionuk.com/2022/01/14/wales-guidance-on-religion-values-and-ethics-published/
16 The following reflects the contents of the websites on 13 January 2022 when they were first published.

purpose of the Guidance is to 'provide additional support on how RVE can be taught within the Humanities Area'.

However, both the Draft Guidance and Curriculum Guidance also stressed the 'holistic' nature of the new curriculum as a whole and state that links need to be made between RVE and all other aspects of the curriculum. The Curriculum Guidance states that it 'emphasises the integral nature of RVE within this Area and outlines the unique and distinct contribution that RVE makes to the Curriculum for Wales'. It mentions various 'disciplinary approaches relevant to RVE' ('religious studies, philosophy, theology, sociology, psychology, and anthropology') and stresses that 'there are also strong relationships between RVE and the other disciplines within Humanities as well as with other Areas'. Both the Draft Guidance and Curriculum Guidance stated that 'curriculum design can be integrated, multidisciplinary, interdisciplinary or disciplinary'.

In my response to the consultation, I argued that clarity was needed on the relationship between RVE and other subjects that make up the Humanities AoLE such as History and Geography: does the fact that it is a statutory requirement mean that more emphasis should be put on links between RVE and other parts of the curriculum or is RVE in the same position in this regard as History, Geography and so on? The reference to the various types of curriculum design also raise questions about what is legally permissible. Would it be permitted, for instance, for a school to devise its Humanities AoLE without reference to RVE if it integrated RVE elsewhere within the curriculum? If a disciplinary approach is taken and RVE is taught separately would this frustrate the 'holistic' intentions of the new curriculum? My recommendation in my submission was that these questions be explicitly addressed in the guidance.

These issues were not explicitly addressed in the Curriculum Guidance. However, it is notable that there the retention of the 'disciplinary' option is the only reference in the Guidance that goes against an integrated and holistic approach. It states that schools are asked to consider 'how RVE will work best within the Humanities Area'. The Guidance is explicit that the first step is to 'consider the Humanities statements of what matters, which contribute to learners realising the four purposes of the curriculum' and then to 'consider the statements of what matters in other Areas where RVE may be able to contribute to learning'.

The Curriculum Guidance does provide some further clarity on the relationship between what will now be the Standing Advisory Councils on RVE and particular schools. The Guidance states that 'RVE is a locally determined subject' with an agreed syllabus being determined at local authority level. It states that 'the agreed syllabus is the first point of reference for

RVE provision in schools' However, it then says that local authorities could 'adopt or adapt this guidance as their agreed syllabus' if they so wish. This is strengthened in the Legislation Summary which states that 'the statutory RVE guidance has been written as the basis for the agreed syllabus'. Even if the local authority does not adopt or adapt the Curriculum Guidance they must nevertheless make sure that the agreed syllabus recognises and reflects the principles laid out in it 'in order to create balance and maintain coherence across the Curriculum for Wales'. And where Standing Advisory Councils on RVE depart from the Curriculum Guidance, it will be open to schools to follow the national guidance rather than the local version.

The Legislation Summary also provides that 'the agreed syllabus is not designed to be a scheme of work, but rather a helpful guide and legal reference point for schools to support them in designing an appropriate and relevant curriculum for their learners which includes RVE within the Humanities Area'. It states that the new curriculum 'is based on the principle of subsidiarity and, as such, each agreed syllabus should recognise and reflect the autonomy of each school and setting in realising its own curriculum'. It points out that 'it will ultimately be the responsibility of the provider to ensure that non-denominational RVE is provided pluralistically'.

The Curriculum Guidance therefore raises once more the question of whether there is a need for Standing Advisory Councils on RVE at all given that they and schools are expected to follow the nationally imposed Curriculum Guidance and that decisions as to content are made at a school level.

The Opt out for Teachers

The questions I raised in the consultation response about the relationship between RVE and other humanities subjects are particularly important given that section 59(3) and (4) of the School Standards and Framework Act 1998 have been left unaltered. These provide that teachers cannot 'be required to give religious education' nor is he or she to 'receive any less remuneration or be deprived of, or disqualified for, any promotion or other advantage...by reason of the fact that he does or does not give religious education'. In my submission, I argued that it needs to be clarified whether the reference to 'religious education' here extends to RVE and if it does, the guidance needs to explain how this right will operate in practice given that RVE is likely to be subsumed within Humanities lessons in some schools and is to be taught as part of a 'holistic' curriculum. This makes teachers opting out of teaching RVE more difficult than opting out of RE at present which tends to be taught as a discreet subject. Both pieces of guidance published in January 2022 are silent on this matter.

The Nature of RVE in Schools with a Religious Character

These questions are even more pressing in the context of RVE in schools with a religious character. In my submission to the consultation, I pointed out that it is unclear how teaching RVE within the Humanities AoLE or within the holistic curriculum as a whole would work where there are two different forms of RVE potentially being taught (one according to the agreed syllabus, one according to trust deeds or ethos). Furthermore, where the RVE conforms to the school's trust deeds or religious ethos, it may be questioned how this denominational RVE is meant to interact and infuse with other aspects of the Humanities and other AoLEs. This could have the effect of the whole curriculum being taught through the denominational lens. The Draft Guidance defines RVE as being pluralistic:

> RVE in the curriculum is not about making learners religious or non-religious; its teaching therefore must promote openness, impartiality and respect for others through an objective, critical and pluralistic approach.

However, as I pointed out in my submission to the consultation, there is nothing in the Act that requires RVE taught in accordance with the school's trust deeds or religious ethos to meet this standard. Indeed, RVE is only permitted to be taught according to the school's trust deeds or ethos where the agreed syllabus RVE does not accord with the trust deed provisions or tenets.[17]

The Curriculum Guidance includes a similar and equally problematic paragraph:

> In the Curriculum for Wales RVE is objective, critical and pluralistic, both in content and pedagogy; it is not about making learners 'religious' or 'non-religious'. The expression 'objective, critical and pluralistic' comes from European Convention on Human Rights case law. The Curriculum and Assessment (Wales) Act 2021 ensures that all learners must be offered opportunities through RVE to engage with different religions and non-religious philosophical convictions in their own locality and in Wales, as well as in the wider world.

---

17 Curriculum and Assessment (Wales) Act 2021, Schedule 1, paras 3(4) and 4(30).

The final sentence in the paragraph quoted here is particularly suspect. It is questionable whether schools of a religious character are required to include opportunities to engage with different religions and non-religious philosophical convictions, where they are permitted to teach according to their trust deeds or ethos. The Legislation Summary similarly assumes that the requirement that RVE engages with different religions and non-religious philosophical convictions applies to all schools. It states that the change in name to RVE 'reflects the expanded scope of religious education (RVE) and ensures the legislation itself is clear that RVE includes non-religious philosophical views'.

However, this is not my reading of the legislation. With the exception of RVE for sixth formers, which is explicitly defined in section 61 as needing to reflect 'a range of non-religious philosophical convictions', the requirement to reflect a range of 'non-religious philosophical convictions' only applies to RVE taught in accordance with the agreed syllabus. There is no suggestion in the legislation that this is an element that schools with a religious character cannot opt out of where they are permitted to teach according to their trust deeds or ethos. Such denominational teaching on religion would not need to include non-religious philosophical convictions, where teaching this would be contrary to the trust deeds or ethos of schools of a religious character.

The reference to opportunities for learners is also questionable given that the choice as to whether to receive denominational teaching or agreed syllabus rests in schools with a religious character with the parents not the learners.

Other than this, the guidance published in January 2022 provides little clarity on the nature of RVE in schools with a religious character. The Curriculum Guidance simply states that 'additional guidance relating to RVE for voluntary-aided schools and settings has been produced by the Church in Wales and the Catholic Education Service with funding from Welsh Government'. It does not, however, link to that Guidance. The Legislation Summary simply provides a recap of the law on the matter.

The Definition of RVE

The name RVE itself also continues to be confusing. The Draft Guidance states that the name change was needed 'to more accurately reflect the broad scope of the subject's pluralistic requirement, and position within the Humanities Area of Learning and Experience'. Yet, it then went on to list 'values and ethics' as one of seven lenses 'through which to view RVE concepts'. As I argued in my submission, at the very least, it would aid clarity if a different label to 'values and ethics' were used for the sixth lens.

Unfortunately, however, confusion still exists in the Curriculum Guidance in that the RVE lens remains divided into a number of sub lenses through which the RVE concepts can be viewed and explored and the sixth sub lens remains 'values and ethics', which is concerned with 'how and why people make moral choices and how this influences their actions'.

The root of the problem is the inclusion of the words 'values and ethics' in the name for the new subject. Unlike the terms 'beliefs', 'worldviews' or 'convictions', 'values and ethics' are not terms that have been legally defined or used in court decisions. They also denote particular characteristics of all religious and non-religious worldviews. As we will see, the Legislation Summary continues to adopt the definitions expressed in the case law of the European Court of Human Rights, but this simply underlines that it would have been preferable to adopt the same terms or synonyms used in the case law rather than the words 'values and ethics'.

The Definition of Religion

Confusion also remains as to the definition of the terms 'religious traditions' and 'non-religious philosophical convictions' as found in the new section 375A of the Education Act 1996 which requires the agreed syllabus to 'reflect the fact that the religious traditions in Wales are in the main Christian while taking account of the teaching and practices of the other principal religions represented in Wales' as well as 'the fact that a range of non-religious philosophical convictions are held in Wales'. Leaving aside the problematic retention of the 'in the main Christian' requirement, the Draft Guidance complicated matter by providing a threefold definition for which it provides no authority or citation. It stated:

> We regard a religion to have the following characteristics:
>
> - the followers have a belief in a supreme being (the concept of a supreme being includes but is not limited to the longstanding concept of a monotheistic Christian God);
> - the followers take part in worship of that supreme being, that is acts or practices in which they give expression to their belief in the supreme being and show reverence for, or veneration of, it; and,
> - the organisation advances that religion through its activities.

The notion that a religion includes both the followers and the organisation itself is unproblematic. However, the formulation of religion as requiring belief and worship reflects a legal definition of religion that only applied in particular circumstances and now has been superseded.[18] I suggested in my submission that it would be preferable either to leave religion undefined or to include a sentence similar to the summary provided or the definition, found in section 10 of the Equality Act 2010 which simply states that 'religion means any religion'.

The question of the definition of religion is not raised in the Curriculum Guidance. The Legislation Summary states that the definition of religion continues to be that 'clarified in section 375A of the Education Act 1996 (the 1996 Act) which refers to religious traditions'. The Legislation Summary concludes that 'what must be included is a range of different religions'. It would have been wise to leave the matter at that but instead the document goes on to provide a list of world religions and denominations within them, which it says that 'courts have decided a belief is a philosophical conviction within the meaning of the ECHR'. This is confusing given that the list provided is of religious groups. The Summary states that 'these are just examples of some religions and not an exhaustive list'. It is questionable whether the list of examples provided (and its references to the names Strasbourg decisions provided without citations) is necessary or indeed helpful.

The final guidance is much clearer than the draft. The absence of extended and, in some respects, outdated discussion of definition issues is to be welcomed. However, the list of examples given is unlikely to be helpful and may encourage a 'tick box' approach that is contrary to the new curriculum and the approach of the Europeans Court of Human Rights which it clings to.

The Definition of Philosophical Convictions

In terms of 'non-religious philosophical convictions', the Draft Guidance questionably noted that this 'relates to the Value and Ethics element in the title to this new subject' and that under the 2021 Act, the term 'philosophical convictions' is within the meaning of Article 2 of the First Protocol to the European Convention on Human Rights (which they refer to as A2P1, making it sound a little like a *Star Wars* droid). The Draft Guidance noted that 'Article 9 and A2P1 apply to the same range of views/beliefs/convictions'. It was therefore confusing that the Draft Guidance then treated them as two definitions. It appeared to give separate discussion of the term 'philosophical convictions' under Article 2 of the First Protocol first before selectively quoting from domestic and Strasbourg Article 9 decisions. In my submission,

---

18 See further Russell Sandberg, 'Clarifying the Definition of Religion under English Law: The Need for a Universal Definition?' (2018) 20 *Ecclesiastical Law Journal* 132.

I argued that it would have been preferable to begin by stating clearly that the reference to non-religious philosophical convictions reflects the meaning attached to convictions and beliefs under the ECHR as a whole, and that this is understood to require a worldview rather than a mere opinion: views that attain a certain level of cogency, seriousness, cohesion and importance. Providing further details as to the definition along the lines that the Draft Guidance included with selective references to the international and domestic case laws is unnecessary.

Unfortunately, while the January 2022 guidance makes some welcome corrections and omissions, it continues to suffer from some of the defects of the Draft Guidance in terms of confusing rather than aiding clarity especially through the provision of provide selective references to the international and domestic case laws. The Curriculum Guidance is silent on the matter but the Legislation Summary notes that that references to 'non-religious philosophical convictions' in the Curriculum and Assessment (Wales) Act are 'linked to the term "philosophical convictions" within the meaning of Article 2 Protocol 1 of the European Convention on Human Rights (A2P1)'. The Summary states that this means that 'the RVE provided in accordance with the Act must be compatible with A2P1 in that it must include teaching on philosophical convictions within the meaning of A2P1'. However, as argued above, the reference to reflecting non-religious philosophical convictions only applies to agreed syllabus RVE and the optional RVE taught to sixth formers. The Legislation Summary seems to accept this by stating that 'the Act makes it explicit that any agreed syllabus for RVE must reflect both religious beliefs and also non-religious beliefs which are philosophical convictions within the meaning of A2P1'.

The Legislation Summary does provide some useful information about definitional matters. It notes that the 'Act refers to "non-religious philosophical convictions" and not "philosophical convictions"' because 'religious philosophical convictions are already covered by the section that refers to "religions"'. It then states that non-religious philosophical convictions include 'beliefs such as humanism, atheism and secularism' but that this 'is not an exhaustive list but just examples of the sort of beliefs that are within scope of RVE'. It insists that 'these changes make explicit what the law already requires in respect of pluralistic RVE'.

The Legislation Summary further states that Council of Europe recommendations are helpful in this regard before stating that courts have held that non-religious philosophical convictions are 'not synonymous with the terms "opinions" and "ideas"' but rather 'denotes views that attain a certain level of cogency, seriousness, cohesion and importance'. These statements are useful but it would arguably have been wise to state that the definition given under the ECHR is basically that a worldview is required. The language used in the letter by Kirsty Williams in May 2018 which stated that non-religious beliefs 'must be analogous to a religious belief' would have been helpful here and it is unclear why the references to being analogous have been dropped given that Legislation Summary states that the definition provided in the 2021 Act is 'what the law already requires'.[19]

However, despite these shortcomings, had Legislation Summary stopped there then it would have been a clear improvement on the Draft Guidance. Unfortunately, the Legislation Summary then follows the Draft Guidance by confusing matters significantly by providing a brief list, name-checking Strasbourg and domestic decisions, of 'some examples where the courts have decided a belief is a philosophical conviction within the meaning of the ECHR' while also stressing that these 'are just examples and not an exhaustive list'. This list shows how problematic the adoption of the Strasbourg jurisprudence is in this area since the terms have been defined widely by Strasbourg in the cases cited in the guidance to include principled opposition to military service and veganism. While these should no doubt be taught in schools, they are not equivalent to and should not replace the teaching of systems of non-religious worldviews. The uncritical adoption of the human rights jurisprudence means that it will also be difficult to determine groups of persons who represent non-religious philosophical convictions on the Standing Advisory Committees: should they really include a representative of vegans alongside a member of Humanists UK? The Guidance confuses rather than clarifies the issue. Again, it is questionable whether the level of detail provided is necessary or helpful.

The Position of Sixth Formers

The Draft Guidance and Legislation Summary both include a questionable paragraph on the position of sixth-formers. It states that:

> Section 61 of The Act does not prevent a school from imposing a requirement that all pupils in its sixth form undertake compulsory RVE classes; nor does it prevent a school that adopts this approach from providing compulsory sixth form RVE that accords with the school's trust deeds, or the tenets of its religion, or religious denomination ('denominational RVE'). The content of such denominational RVE remains a matter for the schools.

---

19 A similar problem has arisen in discrimination law which originally protected 'similar philosophical beliefs' but the reference to 'similar' was removed in the Equality Act 2006.

As I noted in my response to the consultation on the Draft Guidance, there is no legal basis for this. The provisions in the Schedules to the Act only apply to education up to the age of 16.[20] They do not apply to sixth formers. The matter of RVE for sixth formers is now solely regulated by section 61 in relation to maintained schools. Section 61 states that in maintained schools, RVE for sixth formers is 'provided at the school for pupils who request it'. This means that, contrary to what the Legislation Summary states, it cannot be compulsory: it cannot be provided for those who do not request it. Technically, section 61 provides an 'opt in' rather than an 'opt out' approach and this underscores that RVE cannot be compulsory.

Furthermore, section 61 provides that RVE for sixth formers in maintained schools must reflect the two facts – 'that the religious traditions in Wales are mainly Christian, while taking account of the teaching and practices of the other principal religions represented in Wales' and 'that a range of non-religious philosophical convictions are held in Wales'. It therefore does not provide that such RVE could accord with trust deeds or a school's ethos if the school's ethos does not reflect those facts. Under section 61, RVE may only accord with such denominational teaching provided that it reflects the facts stated above. The January 2022 Regulations are based on the assumption that the two facts apply to schools with a religious character in relation to children under the age of 16 and suggests that they do not apply to sixth formers. Yet, on my reading the legislation states the reverse: the two facts do not apply to those who do not follow an agreed syllabus under the Schedules to the Act but section 61 makes it plain that they do apply to sixth formers.

This underlines that the Guidance on the position of sixth-formers – as with the other matters discussed in this chapter – needs to be re-written. It is unfortunate that the guidance remains convoluted. Although the guidance on RVE published in January 2022 is a marked improvement on the draft, it still raises more questions than it answers and is unlikely to provide clarity to those to which it is addressed.

---

20 Sections 1, 9, 19 and 26 state that Parts 1 and 2 of the Act do not apply to those over compulsory school age. This includes sections 24 (3), 29(3)(b) and 30(6)(b). This means that Schedule 1 to the Act does not apply to those over compulsory school age because it is stated that it applies for the purpose of these named sections. Part 5 on post-compulsory education in maintained schools (which includes section 61) does not make reference to Schedule 1 and repeats definitions found in Schedule 1 which underlines that the arrangements in Schedule 1 do not apply to those over compulsory school age.

Chapter 12

CONCLUSION

The law on religion in schools in England is the historical product of the State supplementing and subsiding the original central role played by churches and voluntary groups in education, the compromises reached in the 1940s and the conservative nostalgic concerns that were ingrained into legislation in the 1980s. The law on religious education in Wales is now the product of the wider desire to introduce a Curriculum for Wales that rejects the standardisation and bureaucracy of the National Curriculum. The reforms to what is now RVE were moulded by the way in which various papers and consultations were framed, which questions were asked and which were not and how the Welsh Government chose to summarise and respond to the responses made. Taking a chronological approach to both the wider history of the law relating to the teaching of religion in schools and the particular legislative history of the Curriculum and Assessment (Wales) Act 2021 has shown that pragmatism and making compromises have underlined the approach of the determined architects behind major reforms (Rab Butler and Kirsty Williams) and have been have been vital to the development of the law.[1]

This is an area of law where governments have been wary of treading and where reform of the teaching of religion has only come about as a necessary but inconvenient by-product of wider education reform, be that the tripartite system of secondary education in the 1940s, the National Curriculum in the 1980s or the Curriculum for Wales today. Even when reform has been reluctantly acted upon, deference to organised religions and local decision-making has often meant that some matters have remained off the table. This is an area of law, where, to change metaphors, we have never begun from scratch with a blank sheet of paper. A historical approach also underlines that similar concerns, debates and solutions have echoed through the decades and indeed

---

1 This is a common theme in legal history works and has been underlined in scholarship which has explored legal reforms from the vantage point of reform movements. For an excellent example see Sharon Thompson, *Quiet Revolutionaries: The Married Women's Association and Family Law* (Hart, 2022).

centuries. This is true of educational reform generally. The statement that 'education in the future must be a process of gradually widening horizons from the family to the local community, from the community to the nation, and from the nation to the world' may come from the 1943 White Paper on 'Educational Reconstruction',[2] but it also provides an apt summary of the approach of the new Curriculum for Wales today.

However, although there is a significant amount of continuity, the reforms discussed in this book have all left important marks. This will be true of the new approach that will be ushered in under the Curriculum and Assessment (Wales) Act 2021, which reflects a more pluralistic approach with the autonomy of schools increased. However, the level of school autonomy is especially pronounced in relation to schools with a religious character to such an extent that the pluralistic requirement is likely to be lost there and their legal position still largely resembles the position under the old law. Although the new Welsh legal framework represents a considerable advance, the Welsh Government has not been bold enough with respect of the position of local authorities and schools with a religious character. There also remains troubling areas of confusion which are likely to lead to conservative interpretations of the new law. These relate to definitional issues, most notably the retention of the explicit mention to Christianity, and the preservation of the teacher opt out which makes little sense in the context of a holistic curriculum.

These problems could have been easily overcome and can be overcome if England (and indeed other jurisdictions) want to reform their laws following the Welsh example – and there remain strong reasons for doing this. The English approach which clings to the outmoded label of RE and is even more unclear about the inclusion of non-religious beliefs is unlikely to be fully immune from any human rights challenges. Should England or others seek to follow Wales then they would be advised to also reform the role of local authority bodies, to use the formula 'religion or belief' as established in human rights discourse and norms and to ensure that pluralistic teaching on religion is compulsory in schools with a religious character and that any denominational teaching on religion is in addition rather than instead of such teaching. This is crucial in ensuring that younger generations are literate and sensitive in relation to religion or belief matters.

Yet, reform of religious education alone is not sufficient. The Curriculum and Assessment (Wales) Act 2021 leaves untouched the law on religious

---

2 Quoted in Gary McCulloch, *Educational Reconstruction: The 1944 Education Act and the Twenty-First Century* (Woburn Press, 1994), 176.

worship despite a public petition on the matter.³ The Committee considered that the Bill was an inappropriate vehicle for such change and Kirsty Williams stated that it would be a matter for a future Senedd term.⁴ Yet, the law on religious worship in schools in England and Wales is arguably more outmoded as the law on religious education was. Private Members Bills have been proposed in the Westminster Parliament on the issue but to date they have had no success. This is regrettable. It is questionable that it is human rights complaint in terms of the freedom to hold non-religious beliefs and the rights of the child. It has also been suggested that the letter of the law is followed even less in practice in relation to worship than education.

There is a need for the Westminster Parliament to reconsider these issues.⁵ Reform of the law in this area should be based upon five principles. First, the law should ensure that the composition of decision-making bodies on religious education and worship (such as SACREs) and the content of religious education and worship reflect the full ambit of freedom of religion or belief and that a pluralistic and critical approach is adopted. Second, there is a need to make such pluralistic teaching on religion or belief compulsory in all schools including those with a religious character.⁶ Third, the law should then enable schools with a religious character to teach denominational religious education in addition to this as a separate subject, with a right to opt out by parent and pupils who are legally competent. Fourth, there is a need to reform the requirement for religious worship to require that all schools provide for the spiritual development of their learners, reflecting freedom of reli-

---

3 https://business.senedd.wales/mgIssueHistoryHome.aspx?IId=18959
4 Welsh Parliament Children, Young People and Education Committee, *Curriculum and Assessment (Wales) Bill: Committee Stage 1 Report* (2020), para 637.
5 The Schools Bill 2022, introduced into the House of Lords in May 2022, may provide for an opportunity for such reconsideration. The Bill, as introduced, does not make any significant changes to the law on religious education and worship in schools. It does, however, deal issues concerning schools with a religious character in England. It extends the definition of 'independent educational institutions' so to include many unregistered faith schools and so subject them to a regulatory scheme similar to that of independent schools. In increasing the regulation of Academies, it restates the position on religious worship and religious education in Academies with a religious character. Consideration of the Bill, therefore, could and should provide opportunity for wider discussion of the law on religion in schools and for amendments to be tabled: Russell Sandberg, 'The Schools Bill 2022: Some Initial Observations', *Law and Religion UK* (16 May 2022) https://lawandreligionuk.com/2022/05/16/the-schools-bill-2022-some-initial-observations/
6 There is an argument that the syllabus of this should be agreed nationally or at school level rather than by local SACREs.

gion or belief (including the freedom not to hold a religion or belief) through collective assemblies which should take place at least weekly and which, as now, can include groups or ages of learners at a time rather than the whole school. Fifth, the law should then permit schools with a religious character to make provision for denominational worship but this should be in addition to the requirement laid out in the fourth principle. These principles show how there remains unfinished business in Wales too notwithstanding the radical advances made in pursuance of the new Curriculum for Wales.

Although 2020–21 will always be primarily remembered for the Covid-19 pandemic and the increased recognition of the role of the Welsh Government in combating that, 2021 in Wales will also be as historically important as 1944 and 1988 were in terms of ground breaking educational reform that included significant reform of the law relating to the place of religion in schools. How that law is implemented remains to be seen. There are clear shortcomings and risks as well as pieces of unfinished business. However, overall, there is much other nations (not least England) can learn from the Curriculum and Assessment (Wales) Act 2021.

BIBLIOGRAPHY

Leighton Andrews, *Ministering for Education: A Reformer Reports* (Parthian, 2014).
Mark Bailey, *After the Black Death: Economy, Society and the Law in Fourteenth Century England* (Oxford University Press, 2021).
Michael Barner, *The Making of the 1944 Education Act* (Continuum, 2000).
Leslie Bash and David Coulby (eds), *The Education Reform Act: Competition and Control* (Cassell, 1989).
Alan Brine and Mark Chater, 'How Did We Get Here?' The Twin Narratives in Mark Chater (ed), *Reforming RE: Power and Knowledge in a Worldviews Curriculum* (John Catt, 2020), 21.
Anna Buchanan, 'The Law on Collective Worship in Welsh Schools – A Critical Study' (Cardiff University, Unpublished LLB Dissertation, 2008).
Lord Butler, *The Art of the Possible: The Memoirs of Lord Butler* (Revised ed, Penguin, 1973).
Mark Chater (ed), *Reforming RE: Power and Knowledge in a Worldviews Curriculum* (John Catt, 2020).
Charles Clarke and Linda Woodhead, *A New Settlement Revised: Religion and Belief in Schools* (Westminster Faith Debates Pamphlet, 2018).
Terence Copley, *Worship, Worries and Winners: Worship in the Secondary School after the 1988 Act* (Church House, 1989).
Terence Copley, *Spiritual Development in the State School* (University of Exeter Press, 2002).
Terrence Copley, *Indoctrination, Education and God* (SPCK, 2005).
Terence Copley, *Teaching Religion* (2nd ed, University of Exeter Press, 2008).
William Cornish et al., *Law and Society in England 1750–1950* (2nd ed, Hart, 2019).
Edwin Cox and Josephine M. Cairns, *Reforming Religious Education: The Religious Clauses of the 1988 Education Reform Act* (Kogan Page, 1989).
Frank Cranmer and Russell Sandberg, 'A Critique of the Decision in Conisbee that Vegetarianism is not a Belief' (2020) 22 (1) *Ecclesiastical Law Journal* 36.
Peter Cumper, 'School Worship: Praying for Guidance' [1998] *European Human Rights Law Review* 1.
Peter Cumper and Alison Mawhinney, *Collective Worship in Schools: An Evaluation of Law and Policy in the UK* (AHRC Network Report, 2015).
Peter Cumper and Alison Mawhinney (eds), *Collective Worship and Religious Observance in Schools* (Peter Lang, 2018).
Norman Doe, *The Law of the Church in Wales* (University of Wales Press, 2002).
Norman Doe (ed), *A New History of the Church in Wales: Governance and Ministry, Theology and Society* (Cambridge University Press, 2020).
Gareth Evans, *A Class Apart: Learning the Lessons of Education in Post-Devolution Wales* (Ashley Drake Publishing, 2015).

C. H. S. Fifoot, *Frederic William Maitland* (Harvard University Press, 1971).
Michael Flude and Merril Hammer (eds), *The Education Reform Act 1988: Its Origins and Implications* (Falmer Press, 1990).
John Harrington, Barbara Hughes-Moore and Erin Thomas, 'Towards a Welsh Health Law: Devolution, Divergence and Values' (2021) 72(S1) *Northern Ireland Legal Quarterly* 62.
Mark Hill, Russell Sandberg, Norman Doe and Christopher Grout, *Religion and Law in the United Kingdom* (3rd ed, Kluwer Law International, 2021).
Anthony Howard, *RAB: The Life of R A Butler* (Jonathan Cape, 1987).
Myriam Hunter-Henin (ed), *Law, Religious Freedom and Education in Europe* (Routledge, 2012).
Gareth Elwyn Jones, *Controls and Conflicts in Welsh Secondary Education 1889–1944* (University of Wales Press, 1982).
Gareth Elwyn Jones, *Which Nation's Schools? Direction and devolution in Welsh Education in the Twentieth Century* (University of Wales Press, 1990).
Gareth Elwyn Jones and Gordon Wynne Roderick, *A History of Education in Wales* (University of Wales Press, 2003).
Samantha Knights, *Freedom of Religion, Minorities and the Law* (Oxford University Press, 2007).
Denis Lawton (ed), *The Education Reform Act: Choice and Control* (Hodder & Stoughton, 1989).
Gary McCulloch, *Educational Reconstruction: The 1944 Education Act and the Twenty-First Century* (Woburn Press, 1994).
James Murphy, *The Education Act 1870: Text and Commentary* (David & Charles, 1973).
Robert C. Palmer, *English Law in the Age of the Black Death 1348–1381: A Transformation of Governance and Law* (University of North Carolina Press, 1993).
Frederick Pollock and Frederic W. Maitland, *The History of English Law* (2nd ed, vol 1, Cambridge University Press, 1968 [1898]).
Eric E. Rich, *The Education Act 1870: A Study of Public Opinion* (Longmans, 1970).
Russell Sandberg, *Law and Religion* (Cambridge University Press, 2011).
Russell Sandberg, *Religion, Law and Society* (Cambridge University Press, 2014).
Russell Sandberg, 'Clarifying the Definition of Religion under English Law: The Need for a Universal Definition?' (2018) 20 *Ecclesiastical Law Journal* 132.
Russell Sandberg, 'Religion in Schools in Wales' *Law and Religion UK* (4 October 2019). http://www.lawandreligionuk.com/2019/10/04/religion-in-schools-in-wales/.
Russell Sandberg, 'Is the National Health Service a Religion?' (2020) 22 *Ecclesiastical Law Journal* 343.
Russell Sandberg, 'Radical Reform of "Religion, Values and Ethics" in Welsh Schools' *Law and Religion UK* (6 May 2020). http://www.lawandreligionuk.com/2020/05/06//.
Russell Sandberg, 'Religion, Values and Ethics under the Curriculum and Assessment (Wales) Bill' *Law and Religion UK* (9 July 2020). https://www.lawandreligionuk.com/2020/07/09/religion-values-and-ethics-under-the-curriculum-and-assessment-wales-bill/.
Russell Sandberg, 'Report on the New Welsh Curriculum and the Teaching of Religion' *Sandberg's Subversive Scribblings* (4 December 2020). htttp://sandberglaw.wordpress.com/2020/12/04/report-on-the-new-welsh-curriculumand-and-the-teaching-of-religion.
Russell Sandberg, *Religion and Marriage Law: The Need for Reform* (Bristol University Press, 2021).

Russell Sandberg, *Subversive Legal History: A Manifesto for the Future of Legal Education* (Routledge, 2021).

Russell Sandberg, 'Why the Religion Provisions in the Curriculum and Assessment (Wales) Bill Need Amending' *Law and Religion UK* (25 February 2021). https://lawandreligionuk.com/2021/02/25/why-the-religion-provisions-in-the-curriculum-and-assessment-wales-bill-need-amending/.

Russell Sandberg, 'Wales: Guidance on Religion, Values and Ethics Published' *Law and Religion UK* (14 January 2022). https://lawandreligionuk.com/2022/01/14/wales-guidance-on-religion-values-and-ethics-published/.

Russell Sandberg, 'The Schools Bill 2022: Some Initial Observations', *Law and Religion UK* (16 May 2022). https://lawandreligionuk.com/2022/05/16/the-schools-bill-2022-some-initial-observations/.

Russell Sandberg and Anna Buchanan, 'Religion, Regionalism and Education in the United Kingdom: Tales from Wales,' in Myriam Hunter-Henin (ed), *Law, Religious Freedoms and Education in Europe* (Ashgate, 2012), 107.

Russell Sandberg and Norman Doe, 'The Strange Death of Blasphemy' (2008) 71(6) *Modern Law Review* 971.

Sharon Thompson, *Quiet Revolutionaries: The Married Women's Association and Family Law* (Hart, 2022).

Kyriaki Topidi, *Law and Religious Diversity in Education* (Routledge, 2020).

INDEX

Page numbers with 'n' indicate a footnote on the corresponding page.

Academies 37, 37–38n5
advisory councils 75, 78, 80
agreed syllabus 19–20, 23–25, 28, 31–33, 39–42, 63, 70–7278, 80, 84–85, 88–89, 94, 99–100, 103
Agreed Syllabus Conferences 40, 60, 63, 69–70
Anglo-Saxon period 7
Areas of Learning and Experiences (AoLEs) 56, 59, 75
Attorney-General v Cullum 9, 10

Baroness Emily Blatch 32
Baroness Caroline Cox 28, 32, 47
Baroness Gloira Hooper 29
bipartite system 17
Bishop of London 29
Board of Education 17–18
Bruce, Knight 9–10
Bryce Commission 14
Butler, Richard Austen (Rab) 5, 16–19, 22, 25, 27
Butler Act: *see* Education Act 1944

Catholic Church 21
Catholic Education Service 65, 84, 91, 100
Catholic schools 20
charity schools 8
Children, Young People and Education Committee 79, 83
Children's Commissioner for Wales 73, 85
children's rights 85
Christian character 30, 33–34, 44
Christian denominations 30, 39, 44, 88
Christian education 18
Christian faith 24–25, 28
Christian worship 28–29, 33

Christianity 25, 27–35, 46–47, 50, 66, 108
Church in Wales 84, 91, 100
Church of England 8–12, 14–15, 18–19, 21, 46, 50; representatives 24, 39; school 17, 20; in Wales 53
Church Schools 21, 25, 27
Churchill, Winston 18, 22
Circular 1/94 '33
Circular 10/94 53, 57–58
civil disobedience 14
collective worship 23, 30–31, 33, 44–45, 47, 80
Commission on RE 64
community schools 37, 37n3, 44
community-controlled schools 38
community-special schools 37, 37n3
conscience clause 5, 9–10, 12, 15
Conservative Party 17
consultation process 59–73; *Consultation on Proposals to Ensure Access to the Full Curriculum for all Learners* 62–67; publication 67; response to White Paper 61–62; RVE 67–73; White Paper 59–61
Council of Europe 103
county schools 22–23, 30
Covid-19 1, 95, 110
Cowper-Temple, William 12
Cowper-Temple clause 12
cross-curriculum responsibilities 56, 62
Curriculum and Assessment (Wales) Act 2021 1–3, 51–52, 67, 73, 93–95, 107–9; Clause 6 75; consideration of amendments 88–89; consideration of general principles and plenary debate on general principles 83–88; passing and followed by Royal Assent 83; plenary consideration of amendments

89–91; RVE and local authorities 78–81; RVE in schools 75–78; Schedules 1 and 2 93–94
'Curriculum for Wales - Summary of Legislation' webpage 96
'Curriculum Framework for Religious Education, A' (2013) 34
'Curriculum Guidance' 96–100, 102–3

Davies, Suzy 88–91
denominational teaching 43
Department of Education 33, 34
discrimination law 48, 66
domestic education laws 37, 46
Donaldson, Graham 55–56
Donaldson Report 51, 55–57
Douglas-Home Conservative Government 5
'Draft Guidance' 96–97, 99–105
'dual' system 12, 14, 19

Earl of Arran 29, 31
ECHR: *see* European Convention on Human Rights
education: experience 7; government expenditure on 8; provision 8, 9, 14; system 6
Education Act 1902 14, 17
Education Act 1918 15
Education Act 1944 5–6, 17–25, 27–29, 32, 42, 45; 55; 50; 31; 54
Education Act 1993 32–33
Education Act 1996 37, 64, 78–80, 94, 101–2
Education After the War 18–19
Education Committee of the Privy Council 8–9
Education Reform Act 1988 6, 27, 29–35, 45, 50, 55
'Educational Reconstruction' 21, 108
educational reforms 18–22, 25, 55, 110
elementary education: *see* primary education
Elementary Education Act 1870 11-15
Elementary Education Act 1880 14
elementary school 12–13, 16
Equality Act 2010 49, 102
Estyn 84
European Convention on Human Rights (ECHR) 50, 61, 99, 101, 103; Article 2 48–49, 68–69, 78–79, 93, 102–3; Article 9 49, 79; rights 83
European Court of Human Rights 69, 102

faith groups 84–85
faith schools 41–43, 68, 90–91
formal education 7–8
Forster, William Edward 11
Forster Act: *see* Elementary Education Act 1870
foundation schools 37–38, 37n3, 41–42, 44, 76, 93
foundation-special schools 37, 37n3
Free Churches 18–19
Free Schools 37, 38n5
free secondary schooling 5
freedom of religion/belief 2, 6, 46, 48, 49-50
funding 5, 8–9, 12, 14, 20, 84

GCSE Subject Content 41
Gladstone Government of Wales Act: 1998 54; 2006 54
grammar schools 7–8, 10, 27
Green Book: *see Education After the War*

Health and Well-being AoLE 67
Higher Elementary Schools 14
Hinsley, Arthur 20
holy orders 10
House of Commons 21
House of Lords 18, 24, 27–30, 47
Howard, Anthony 13, 15, 17–19, 21, 25
human rights 46, 48, 50, 104, 108–9
Human Rights Act 199) 49, 57, 60, 69, 79
Humanities AoLE 59–60, 62–64, 67, 71, 75, 96–100

independent schools 37, 37n4, 43, 80, 109
Industrial Revolution 7
inquiry-based learning 93
Interim Executive Board of X School v Chief Inspector of Education 38n8
international human rights laws 6, 66

Jones, Gareth Elwyn 7

Kenyon-Slaney, William 14
Kenyon-Slaney clause 14
King's Speech 20–21

Labour Government 91
Labour Government Circular (1965) 27
Labour Party 51
Labour Party Education Ministers 54
'Legislation Summary' 96, 98, 100–105
legislative devolution 53–54

INDEX

Lewis, Huw 55
Liberal Democrats 51
local authorities / Local Education Authorities (LEAs)5, 14–15, 17,19-20, 22-24 32, 37–40, 44
Lord Lyndhurst 10
Lord Selborne 24, 25, 28

Macmillan Government 5
maintained schools 37–38, 75, 93, 105
Maitland, Frederic 7
marriage laws 50
meaning of life 42
McCulloch, Gary 22
Miles, Jeremy 51, 95
Millar, Darren 89
Ministry of Education 17
multicultural society 64
multi-faith syllabuses 28

National Assembly for Wales: *see* Welsh Senedd (Welsh Parliament)
National Association of Head Teachers 31
National Curriculum 27, 29–31, 34, 48, 55, 57
National Framework for RE 34
national human rights law 66
National Secular Society 84
National Society 19
non-Conformist Church 21
non-conformists 12, 19
non-denominational agreed syllabus 20, 40
non-departmental public bodies 34
non-religious beliefs 57, 59, 62–64, 68–69, 78–79, 108–9
non-religious philosophical convictions 78–80, 86, 88, 93–94, 99–104
non-religious schools 15
non-religious worldviews 65, 101, 104
non-statutory documents 34, 35
non-statutory programme 48

parental rights 21–22, 48–49, 52, 61–62, 73, 76, 83
pedagogical approach 93
philosophical beliefs 69
pluralism 32, 63
'Pluralistic Requirement' 68–69, 72, 79, 86
political beliefs 69
Poor Law 8

primary education 7–8, 14, 16–17, 22, 54, 75, 87
private venture schools 8

Qualification and Curriculum Development Agency 34
Qualifications and Curriculum Authority 34

R (on the application of E) v JFS Governing Body 38n9
R (on the application of Fox) v Secretary of State for Education 41
R v Secretary of State for Education ex parte R and D 34
RE Council 64–65
Re Ilminster Free School 11
*Re The King's Grammar School, War*wick 10
Relationship and Sexuality Education (RSE) 61–64
religion, definition of 101–2
Religion, Values and Ethics (RVE) 52, 66–73, 75; definition 100–101; denominational 72, 84–85, 91, 99, 104; and local authorities 78–81; non-denominational 84, 89–91, 98; placing within Humanities AoLE 96–99; pluralistic 71–73, 77, 83, 85, 87–88, 90–91, 103; position of sixth-formers 104–5; in schools 75–78, 84, 93, 99–100; syllabus 88, 90; teaching 89
Religion and Worldviews 48, 64–67
religious beliefs 68, 103
religious character 1–2, 38–47, 54–55, 60, 64, 72; schools with 71–73, 84–86, 99–100; schools without 70–71
religious denomination 12, 16, 23–24, 40–43, 45, 64
religious discrimination 49–50
religious diversity 32, 41
Religious Education (RE) 6, 9, 14, 18–19, 24, 28–32; and agreed syllabus 75–77; content 61; denominational 12, 19, 23, 64, 72, 77; law on 5, 107; placing within Humanities 56, 59–60, 62–64; provision 54; pupils excused from 76; renaming 66; in schools with religious character 41–43, 85; in schools without religious character 38–41; teachers for 98–99
Religious Education Council of England and Wales 34
religious freedom 43, 65, 85, 91

Religious Instruction (RI) 9–12, 15, 17–20, 22–25, 27–28
religious leaders 18–19, 21
Religious Studies (RS) 41
religious traditions 45, 64, 69, 78, 86, 101
religious worship 2–3, 5–6, 15, 27–31, 33, 48; provision 54; pupil withdrawn from 76, 95; in schools with religious character 45–46; in schools without religious character 44–45
reserved teachers 23, 42
right to education 48–49, 79
Roderick, Gordon Wynne 7
Royal Assent 83
RSE: *see* Relationship and Sexuality Education
RVE: *see* Religion, Values and Ethics

School Boards 11, 14
School Standards and Framework Act 1998 37, 44, 75–76, 80, 94, 98; Schedule 19 71
Schools Bill 2022 109
school(s): buildings 8, 20–21; inspections 8; types of 8
Schools Curriculum and Assessment Authority 34
secondary education 7, 14, 16–17, 53, 107
secondary schools 18, 22, 95
Secretary of State 80
secularisation 6
Senedd and Elections (Wales) Act2020 54
'single-school' areas 17
Society for Promoting Christian Knowledge 8
Standing Advisory Councils for Religious Education (SACREs) / Standing Advisory Councils/Committees (SACs) 2, 24, 30, 33, 39–40, 44–47, 50, 57, 60, 63, 70, 79, 80, 86-89, 94, 97, 104
Star Wars 102
'subtraction stories' 6
Successful Futures: Independent Review of Curriculum and Assessment Arrangements in Wales 55

Sunday Schools 8, 13, 22, 38
Swann Committee 27

Taylor, Charles 6
technical schools 17
Temple, William 19
Thatcher Government 6, 29, 32
Times, The 18, 20
Times Educational Supplement, The 28
tripartite system 5, 17
trust schools 37n3

United Nations Committee on the Right of the Child 48, 50

'values and ethics' 66, 100–101
voluntary schools 11, 12, 17, 20–23, 44–45, 54
voluntary system 14
voluntary-aided schools 20, 22–23, 41–43, 45, 59, 71–72; agreed syllabus and 86; and religious character 76, 94; RVE for 100
voluntary-controlled schools 20, 22–23, 38, 41–43, 45, 71–73; and religious character 76, 93

Welsh Assembly: see Welsh Senedd (Welsh Parliament)
Welsh Baccalaureate 54
Welsh Government 51–52, 54–55, 57–60, 62–65, 67–72, 107-9; and Guidance for RVE 95–96; 'pluralistic requirement' 77, 79; proposals 87; school trust deeds and 89–90
Welsh Intermediate Act1889 53
Welsh Ministers 70, 80–81, 94–95
Welsh Office 53
Welsh Senedd (Welsh Parliament) 1–3, 51–52, 54, 75, 87, 91
Williams, Kirsty 51, 57, 78, 83–84, 86–87, 90–91, 109
World War I 15
World War II 5, 15–16

www.ingramcontent.com/pod-product-compliance
Lightning Source LLC
Chambersburg PA
CBHW030142170426
43199CB00008B/167